The Cheesecake Factory

The Unofficial Copycat Recipe Cookbook

Copyright

Copyright 2019 New Wave Publishing. All rights reserved under International and Pan-American Copyright Conventions. No rights granted to reproduce this book or portions thereof in any form or manner whatsoever without the express written permission of the copyright owner(s).

Legal Notice

Content in this book is provided "As Is". The authors and publishers provide no guarantees regarding results of any advice or recommendations contained herein. Much of this book is based on personal experiences of the author(s) and anecdotal evidence. Although the author and publisher have made reasonable attempts to for accuracy in the content, they assume no responsibility for its veracity, or for any errors or omissions. Nothing in this book is intended to replace common sense, medical, legal or other professional advice. This book is meant only to be informative and entertaining. Encore Books and its authors shall not be liable in the event of incidental or consequential damages in connection with, or arising out of, the providing of the information offered herein.

Any trademarks, service marks, product names or named features are assumed to be the property of their respective owners, and are used herein for reference purposes only. This book was not prepared, approved, licensed, or endorsed by any of the owners of the trademarks or brand names referred to in this book. There is no implied endorsement for any products or services mentioned in this publication.

Get Free Recipe eBooks!
Cookbook Club

Fabulous Free eBook Cookbooks Every Week!

Our eBooks are FREE For the first few days publication. Be the first to know when new books are published. Our collection includes hundreds of books on topics including healthy foods, diets, food allergy alternatives, gourmet meals, desserts, and easy and inexpensive meals.

Join the mailing list at:
EncoreBookClub.com

Related Copycat Books
Copycat Applebee's Recipes
http://url80.com/copycatapplebee
Copycat Candy Recipes
http://url80.com/copycatcandy
Copycat Appetizers, Vol. 1
http://url80.com/copycatapp1
Copycat Appetizers, Vol. 2
http://url80.com/copycatapp2
Copycat Buca di Deppo Recipes
http://url80.com/copycatbuca
Copycat Dessert Recipes
http://url80.com/copycatdessert
Homemade Copycat Liqueurs
http://url80.com/copycatliqueur
Copycat Olive Garden Recipes
http://url80.com/copycatolive
Copycat Panera Bread Recipes
http://url80.com/copycatpanera
Copycat PF Chang's Recipes
http://url80.com/copycatpfchang
Copycat Smoothies
http://url80.com/csmoothie
Copycat TGI Friday's Recipes
http://url80.com/fridays

Table of Contents

APPETIZERS — 1

Chicken Potsticker's	2
Avocado Eggrolls	3
Fried Macaroni & Cheese	5
Hot Spinach & Cheese Dip	6
Tex-Mex Eggrolls	7
Warm Crab & Artichoke Dip	9
Buffalo Blasts	11
Crispy Brussels Sprouts	12

MAIN COURSE — 13

Thai Coconut-Lime Chicken	14
Truffle-Honey Chicken	15
Chicken Parm Pizza Style	17
White Chicken Chili	19
Sheppard's Pie	21
Baja Chicken Tacos	23
Chicken Riesling	24
Fish Tacos	25
Tuna Poke	26
Factory Burrito Grande	27
Chicken Madeira	29
Chicken Bellagio	31
Chicken & Biscuits	33
Crusted Chicken Romano	35
Famous Factory Meatloaf	36
Orange Chicken	37
Shrimp & Chicken Gumbo	39
Hibachi Steak	40
Spicy Cashew Chicken	41
Carne Asada Steak	43

CHEESECAKES — 45

- COFFEE & CREAM CHOCOLATE SUPREME — 46
- ORIGINAL FACTORY CHEESECAKE — 47
- CINNABON CINNAMON SWIRL CHEESECAKE — 49
- REESE'S PEANUT BUTTER CHEESECAKE — 51
- LEMON MERINGUE CHEESECAKE — 54
- CELEBRATION CHEESECAKE — 55
- SALTED CARAMEL CHEESECAKE — 57
- CHOCOLATE HAZELNUT CHEESECAKE — 59
- OREO DREAM EXTREME CHEESECAKE — 60
- TOASTED MARSHMALLOWS S'MORES GALORE — 63
- GODIVA CHOCOLATE CHEESECAKE — 65
- ULTIMATE RED VELVET CHEESECAKE — 67
- WHITE CHOCOLATE RASPBERRY TRUFFLE — 70
- KEY LIME CHEESECAKE — 73
- CHOCOLATE MOUSSE CHEESECAKE — 75
- TIRAMISU CHEESECAKE — 77
- CARROT CAKE CHEESECAKE — 79
- PUMPKIN PECAN CHEESECAKE — 81

SPECIALTY DESSERTS — 83

- WARM APPLE CRISP — 84
- LYNDA'S FUDGE CAKE — 85
- BLACKOUT CAKE — 87
- CHOCOLATE TOWER TRUFFLE CAKE — 89
- LIMONCELLO CREAM TORTE — 91

Appetizers

Chicken Potsticker's

Prep Time: 5 minutes
Cooking Time: 15 minutes
Servings: 16

Ingredients

- ½ cup red bell pepper, finely chopped (1 small)
- 1 ½ pounds ground chicken
- ½ cup green cabbage, shredded
- 3 medium green onions, chopped (roughly ⅓ cup)
- 1 large egg white
- 2 teaspoon ginger root, chopped
- 1 package round wonton skins (approximately 10 ounces)
- 4 teaspoon soy sauce, low-sodium
- 1 teaspoon sesame oil
- 2 cups chicken broth
- ¼ teaspoon white pepper

Directions

1. Combine the entire ingredients (don't add the wonton skins, soy sauce and broth) together in a large bowl. Brush each wonton skin with water and then place a scant tablespoon of the chicken mixture on middle of the skin. Pinch 5 pleats on each of one half of circle. Fold the circle in half on top of the chicken mixture; pressing the pleated edge to un-pleated edge. Repeat with leftover chicken mixture & skins.
2. Using nonstick cooking spray; lightly coat a 12" skillet and then heat it over medium heat. Work in batches and cook the pot stickers (12 at a time) for a couple of minutes, until turn light brown. Stir in 1 teaspoon of the soy sauce and½ cup of the broth. Cover & cook for 5 more minutes. Uncover & cook until liquid has evaporated, for a minute more. Repeat the same steps with the leftover pot stickers, soy sauce and broth. Serve hot & enjoy.

Avocado Eggrolls

Prep Time: 10 minutes
Cooking Time: 15 minutes
Servings: 16

Ingredients

For Filling:
- 4 avocados, peeled, pitted & mashed
- ½ cup red onion, finely chopped
- Juice of ½ a lemon or to taste
- 3 tablespoon sun dried tomatoes packed in oil, chopped
- ¼ cup cilantro, fresh, chopped
- 1 jalapeno, finely chopped
- Black pepper & salt to taste

For Cashew-Cilantro Sauce:
- 3 teaspoon white vinegar
- ½ teaspoon tamarind pulp
- 1 teaspoon balsamic vinegar
- 4 tablespoon brown sugar
- 1 cup fresh cilantro, chopped
- ½ cup cashews, chopped
- 3-4 garlic cloves
- ¼ cup red onion, chopped
- 1 tablespoon olive oil
- 3-4 tablespoon water
- Black pepper & salt to taste

Additional Ingredients:
- 1 tablespoon all-purpose flour or any of your favorite
- 16 egg roll wrappers
- Oil for frying
- 1 tablespoon water

Directions

For Filling:
1. Combine the entire ingredients together in a large bowl until combined well. Taste & adjust the amount of lemon juice, black pepper or salt, if required; set aside until ready to use.

For Cashew-Cilantro Sauce:
1. Add the entire sauce ingredients together in a blender & blend on high power until completely smooth. Taste & adjust the amount of tang or sweetness per your preference.

To Assemble:
1. In a medium-sized bowl; combined flour with water until a sticky paste like consistency is formed. Now, lay an egg roll wrapper on a clean, flat surface. Put the filling in the middle & fold by sealing the edges using a flour-water mix.
2. Get the other egg rolls ready in the similar pattern.
3. Now, over moderate heat in a deep pot; heat up the oil until hot. Once done; work in batches and add a few egg rolls into the hot oil; fry for a couple of minutes, until turn golden & crispy.
4. Serve warm with the prepared sauce on side. Enjoy.

Fried Macaroni & Cheese

Prep Time: 1 hour
Cooking Time: 45 minutes
Servings: 15

Ingredients

- 1 cup bread crumbs
- 4 ounces block cream cheese
- 1 box elbow Macaroni
- 4 organic eggs, large
- 1 pound block cheddar Cheese
- ½ cup milk
- 1 Jar of tomato sauce
- ½ cup cheese, shredded to sprinkle over the top

Directions

1. Prepare the pasta as per the directions provided by the manufacturer; drain & add it to the pot.
2. Chop up the cream cheese and cheddar cheese into small cubes
3. Combine the cheddar cheese with cream cheese & pasta until the cheese coats the pasta and is completely melted. Set aside at room temperature & let cool until easy to handle with your hands.
4. Form balls from pasta mixture & arrange them on wax paper lined baking sheet. Place in freezer until frozen.
5. Have a bowl of bread crumbs & a bowl with a few eggs mixed with a small amount of milk ready.
6. Take the frozen mac & cheese balls out from the freezer & then dip them into the egg-milk mixture and then into the bread crumbs. For every mac & cheese ball; repeat this step again.
7. Once the entire mac & cheese balls are nicely coated; work in batches and fry them at 350 F in a deep fryer until turn dark brown in color, for 3 to 5 minutes per batch
8. Once done; put a spoon full of the sauce on the bottom of a clean, large plate and arrange the fried mac & cheese balls on top, spoon a small amount of sauce more on the top & sprinkle with the shredded cheese. Serve warm & enjoy.

Hot Spinach & Cheese Dip

Prep Time: 5 minutes
Cooking Time: 10 minutes
Servings: 2

Ingredients

- 1 package spinach, frozen, thawed, chopped & drained (10 ounce)
- ¾ cup mayonnaise
- 1 can water chestnuts, drained & chopped (8 ounce)
- 3 green onions, finely chopped
- 1 container sour cream (16 ounce)
- 2 teaspoon prepared Dijon-style mustard
- 1 package dry vegetable dip mix (1 ounce)

Directions

1. Combine the chopped spinach together with dry vegetable dip mix, mayonnaise, sour cream, green onions, prepared Dijon-style mustard and water chestnuts in a medium-sized bowl.
2. Let chill in a refrigerator for overnight. Serve chilled & enjoy.

Tex-Mex Eggrolls

Prep Time: 20 minutes
Cooking Time: 20 minutes
Servings: 24

Ingredients

For Tex-Mex Egg Rolls:
- 1 tablespoon canola oil
- 1 cup corn
- 2 cups cooked chicken breasts; diced
- 1 cup black beans
- ½ yellow onion; diced
- 1 garlic clove; minced
- 1 Roma tomato; finely diced & dried on paper towel
- ½ cup cheddar cheese shredded
- 1 teaspoon chili powder
- 1 green bell pepper; diced
- 2 tablespoon fresh cilantro, chopped
- 1 teaspoon cumin
- 1 package (24 count) egg roll wrappers
- Canola oil for frying
- ½ teaspoon kosher salt

For Avocado Dipping Sauce:
- ½ avocado
- 8 ounces cream cheese
- A bunch of fresh cilantro
- ¼ cup sour cream

Directions

1. Over high heat in a cast iron skillet; heat up the canola oil and then add in the chicken together with garlic, onion, chili powder, cumin & kosher salt.
2. Give the ingredients a good stir & cook for a minute then turn off the heat. Add in the bell pepper, black beans, cheddar cheese, corn, tomato & fresh cilantro; give everything a good stir again.
3. Add a few tablespoons of the mixture to the center of an egg roll wrapper. Beginning from the bottom left; pull the corner over the meat and then fold the two sides in.
4. Wet the edges & roll it tightly. Now, fill a large pan with the canola oil (approximately an inch) and then heat it up over moderate heat.
5. Work in batches & add a few egg rolls (3 to 4 at a time) into the hot oil. Cook until they turn brown and then place them on a cooling rack or dry them on brown paper bag.

Warm Crab & Artichoke Dip

Prep Time: 10 minutes
Cooking Time: 30 minutes
Servings: 1

Ingredients

- 4 slices Sourdough Baguette, sliced ½" thick
- 1 slice of white bread, minced
- ¼ pound crab meat (backfin or lump)
- 3 ounces cream cheese
- 1 cup heavy cream
- 5 ounces sour cream
- ½ pound crabcake mix
- 6 ounces Artichoke Hearts, drained, cut into ¾" pieces
- ½ fl. ounces olive oil
- 6 ounces Crab & Artichoke Mix
- ½ teaspoon fresh parsley, chopped
- 2 teaspoon buttered breadcrumbs, toasted
- ¼ teaspoon each of old bay seasoning, ground black pepper & cayenne pepper
- 4 ounces mayonnaise
- ½ teaspoon kosher salt

Directions

1. For the Mix: Place the cream cheese and minced bread into a large-sized mixing bowl. Pour the heavy cream over the ingredients; mix well until combined evenly.
2. Add in the mayonnaise, sour cream, cayenne pepper, old bay seasoning, pepper & salt into the mixing bowl; give the ingredients a good stir until combined evenly.
3. Add in the crab meat, artichoke hearts & crabcake mix into the bowl. Gently "fold" into the other ingredients; ensure that you don't break up any large lump pieces of the crab.
4. Transfer the mixture to a clean, large storage container.
5. Cover & store under refrigeration.
6. Now, evenly brush each slice of the bread with some olive oil on both sides. Place the bread into a pan set over medium heat or onto a flat grill; cook until the slices turn lightly golden and crispy.
7. Heat the crab & artichoke dip over medium heat in the sauté pan until warm throughout, stirring frequently.
8. Place the artichoke & crab dip into the small serving bowl. Evenly sprinkle the toasted buttered breadcrumbs on top of the artichoke & crab dip.
9. Slice each piece of grilled bread in half at a slight angle. Place the grilled bread slices and the bowl of crab dip onto a serving platter
10. Sprinkle the freshly chopped parsley on top of the bread & crab dip. Serve and enjoy.

Buffalo Blasts

Prep Time: 5 minutes
Cooking Time: 10 minutes
Servings: 4

Ingredients

- ¼ cup buffalo wing sauce
- 1 rotisserie chicken shredded
- 24 wonton paper
- 1 cup oil plus more for frying pan, if required
- ½ cup shredded mozzarella cheese
- A bottle of sriracha for drizzle sauce

Directions

1. Combine the shredded chicken together with wing sauce & cheese in a medium bowl until combined well.
2. Take the wonton wrapper & fill the center with the prepared chicken filling. Fold like a triangle and ensure that the corner meets the other corner.
3. Now, over moderate heat in a large frying pan; heat up the oil until hot.
4. Place the prepared wonton into the hot oil & fry the first for 2 to 3 minutes; flip over.
5. Place onto a paper towel lined plate. Drizzle with the sriracha; serve immediately & enjoy.

Crispy Brussels Sprouts

Prep Time: 5 minutes
Cooking Time: 20 minutes
Servings: 1

Ingredients

- 1 ounces Brussels sprouts leaves
- 6 ounces Brussels Sprouts, washed, drained well; some of the whole outer leaves removed
- 1 slice of Bacon, cooked crisp & chopped
- A pinch of coarse salt
- 1 ounces maple-butter glaze

Directions

1. Cut the Brussels sprouts into quarters. Over moderate heat in a large pan; heat up the oil & fry until slightly crispy & completely cooked. Remove & place them on paper towels to drain.
2. Now, fry the Brussels sprout leaves for a minute or two, until turn crispy. Remove the leaves & place them on paper towels to drain. Sprinkle a small amount of coarse salt on top of the crispy leaves.
3. Place the quartered Brussels sprouts into a large-sized mixing bowl. Add in the chopped bacon & then evenly drizzle with the Maple Butter Glaze; gently toss. Place them onto into a large bowl or a serving plate.
4. Gently mound the crispy Brussels sprout leaves on top of the quartered Brussels sprouts. Serve hot & enjoy.

Main Course

Thai Coconut-Lime Chicken

Prep Time: 10 minutes
Cooking Time: 15 minutes
Servings: 4

Ingredients

- 1 pound boneless skinless chicken breasts cut into 1" cubes
- ¼ cup sweetened coconut, shredded
- 1 can shiitake mushrooms
- 2 tablespoon soy sauce, low-sodium
- 1 tablespoon fresh ginger-root, minced
- ¼ cup lime juice, freshly squeezed
- 1 pc mango; cut into small chunks
- 3 teaspoon canola oil
- 1 tablespoon honey
- 2 teaspoon sesame oil
- 1 cup light coconut milk
- ½ teaspoon red curry paste
- 1 tablespoon lime peel, grated
- ¼ cup snow peas
- 1 tablespoon fresh cilantro, minced
- ⅛ cup cashew nuts
- 1 tablespoon rice vinegar

Directions

1. Over medium heat in a large skillet; cook the sweetened shredded coconut flakes until almost golden brown, stirring frequently & set aside until ready to use.
2. Combine lime juice with ginger, lime peel, soy sauce, honey and vinegar in a small bowl; set aside. Over moderate heat in a large skillet; heat canola & sesame oils. Sauté chicken 2 minutes, until no longer pink from inside. Add the lime mixture and coconut milk into the pan. Bring everything together to a boil; cook for 2 minutes, stirring frequently. Add in the curry paste and then add in the mushrooms, Snow peas, cashew nuts and mango. Cook for 2 to 3 more minutes, stirring frequently. Sprinkle with the coconut & cilantro.
3. Serve with rice; garnish with Lime wedges & freshly chopped cilantro.

Truffle-Honey Chicken

Prep Time: 15 minutes
Cooking Time: 15 minutes
Servings: 6

Ingredients

- 2-4 chicken breasts
- 1 teaspoon garlic powder
- 2 cup all-purpose flour
- 1 cup buttermilk
- 1 teaspoon paprika
- 2 tablespoon truffle honey
- 1 teaspoon onion powder
- 2 quart vegetable oil
- ½ teaspoon each of ground black pepper & salt or to taste

For Oven Roasted Asparagus:
- A bunch of thin asparagus spears trimmed
- 3 tablespoon olive oil
- 1 tablespoon lemon juice, freshly squeezed
- ½ teaspoon each of ground black pepper & garlic powder
- 1 teaspoon sea salt

Directions

1. Using a plastic wrap; cover the chicken & pound both sides of it lightly with a flat mallet.
2. Add flour together with onion powder, garlic powder, paprika, pepper & salt to a large-sized plastic bag; mix until combined well.
3. Add buttermilk to a shallow plate.
4. Dip the chicken breasts first into the buttermilk and then put them into the bag with the flour; seal & shake until nicely coated.
5. Arrange the coated chicken on a tray or plate; cover with a waxed paper or clean dish towel. Let sit until the flour is a paste-like consistency.
6. Now, fill a large skillet approximately ⅓ to ½ full of the vegetable oil & heat over moderate heat until hot.
7. Work in batches & carefully add the chicken breast to the hot skillet; ensure that you don't overlap the chicken pieces.
8. Cook until both sides of the chicken turn brown, for a couple of minutes. Decrease the heat to low & cover the skillet.
9. Cook until the chicken breast is cooked through, but ensure it's not crispy, for 8 to 10 more minutes.
10. Remove the lid, increase the heat & continue to fry until the chicken turn crispy. Transfer to a plate lined with paper towel or tray or cookie sheet. Serve immediately drizzled with Honey Truffle. Serve with some mashed potatoes & asparagus.

For Oven Roasted Asparagus:
1. Preheat your oven to 425 F.
2. Place the asparagus into a large-sized mixing bowl & drizzle with the olive oil. Toss until nicely coated and then sprinkle with the garlic powder, pepper & salt.
3. Arrange the asparagus in a single layer onto a baking sheet.
4. Bake for 12 to 15 minutes, until just tender. Just before serving; don't forget to sprinkle with the lemon juice.

Chicken Parm Pizza Style

Prep Time: 25 minutes
Cooking Time: 20 minutes
Servings: 4

Ingredients

- 1 teaspoon oregano or marjoram
- 3 tablespoon parmesan cheese
- 1 pound ground chicken
- 3 tablespoon parmesan cheese
- Olive oil for frying (enough to cover the skillet by ½")
- 6 ounces fresh mozzarella, sliced
- ½ teaspoon ground pepper
- 1 teaspoon garlic powder
- ½ cup marinara sauce
- 1 teaspoon salt
- Tomatoes & fresh basil for garnish

For Breading & Egg Wash:
- ½ cup panko crumbs
- 1 egg lightly beaten & combined with 1 tablespoon of water
- ¼ cup flour seasoned with a touch of the above & 2 tablespoon parmesan cheese

For Spicy Honey:
- 1-2 teaspoon spicy chili paste
- ½ cup honey

Directions

1. Line 2 standard-sized pie or cake pans (8" each) with the plastic wrap.
2. Combine the ground chicken together with the seasonings. Divide the chicken in half & pat each half into the prepared pan. Freeze for a couple of hours.
3. Prepare the breading and egg wash. Remove the chicken from refrigerator & dust with the flour, sides and bottom. Brush with the egg wash on top, bottom and sides. Using panko crumbs; cover all sides of the chicken.
4. Over moderate heat in a large pan; heat up the oil until it starts shimmering. Once done; work in batches and add the chicken patties into the hot oil. Fry each side for 3 to 5 minutes, until turn golden. Remove & drain.
5. Preheat your oven to 400 F. Cover each chicken patty with approximately ¼ cup of the marinara (don't add too much of sauce). Cover with the parmesan & then cover with the mozzarella.
6. Arrange them on a large-sized baking sheet and then place them into the preheated oven; bake until the cheese is completely melted, for 8 to 10 minutes. Remove from the oven.
7. Heat the broiler to high. Slide the baking sheet under broiler & broil until the cheese turns golden & is glistening, for a couple of more minutes. Garnish with tomatoes and fresh basil. Serve with a pizza cutter.
8. Mix up the honey & drizzle on top. Feel free to serve over arugula or pasta or even both. Enjoy.

White Chicken Chili

Prep Time: 10 minutes
Cooking Time: 40 minutes
Servings: 4

Ingredients

- ¼ cup green onions, chopped ¼"
- 2 pounds chicken breasts, cut into ¾" pieces
- ¼ cup plus 2 tablespoon canola oil
- 2 cups cooked white rice
- ¾ teaspoon ground black pepper
- 2 tablespoon butter
- ¾ cup Yellow onions, diced ¼"
- 1 tablespoon minced garlic
- ¼ teaspoon ground cumin
- 1 qt. chicken stock
- 2 tablespoon salsa verde
- ¾ teaspoon oregano, dried
- 1 ½ teaspoon garlic-chili paste
- ¾ teaspoon brown sugar
- 1 ½ teaspoon Chipotle Tabasco
- 2 cups Canned White Beans, rinsed & drained
- ½ cup all-purpose flour
- 3 tablespoon sour cream
- ½ cup Green Poblano chilies, roasted, peeled, seeds removed & diced
- 1 ½ teaspoon each of ground cumin, chili powder & kosher salt
- ¼ cup Pico de Gallo

Directions

1. Over moderate heat in a large soup or sauce pot; heat up ¼ cup of the canola oil.
2. Now, in a large-sized mixing bowl; combine the chicken together with the spices.
3. Add the coated chicken into the pot with hot oil & cook until almost cooked through & turn lightly brown.
4. Remove & set the chicken aside.
5. Heat the additional oil and butter in the pot. Add and cook the onions for a couple of minutes, until turn tender.
6. Add garlic & then the chilies into the pot; give the ingredients a good stir & cook for half a minute more.
7. Add flour into the hot pot; stir well & cook for 2 more minutes.
8. Slowly add in the chicken stock & stir the ingredients together until no lumps remain and the mixture is completely smooth.
9. Add in the garlic-chili paste, salsa verde, oregano, Tabasco, cumin and brown sugar into the hot pot. Bring the mixture to a simmer and then add in the almost cooked chicken. Let simmer for 3 to 5 more minutes and then gently stir in the white beans and sour cream.
10. Serve with white rice; garnished with green onions and pico de gallo.

Sheppard's Pie

Prep Time: 10 minutes
Cooking Time: 25 minutes
Servings: 4

Ingredients

- 2 Tbsp. oil, divided
- 12 ounces white mushrooms, sliced thinly
- 8 ounces red wine, divided
- ½ cup carrots, julienned
- 1 large onion, diced
- 2 cloves garlic, minced
- 1 lb. ground meat (turkey, lamb or beef)
- 3-4 sprigs fresh thyme, minced
- 1 cup frozen peas
- 1 tbsp. butter
- 2 tbsp. flour
- 2 tbsp. tomato paste
- 2 tbsp. Worcestershire sauce
- 1 cup chicken or beef stock
- 2 medium zucchini, julienned
- Salt and pepper, to taste
- 6 cups prepared mashed potatoes
- 1 egg, beaten
- 2 tbsp. Parmesan cheese, grated

Directions

1. Lightly coat a large-sized casserole dish with the butter and then preheat your oven to 400 F.
2. In the meantime; heat a tablespoon of oil over medium to high heat in a large skillet until hot. Once done; add & sauté the sliced mushrooms for a minute or two, until soft.
3. Add 2 ounces of red wine; scraping and stirring the pan frequently. Bring it to a simmer and continue to cook until the liquid is reduced, for 5 more minutes.
4. Remove the mushrooms & liquid from the pan; set aside. Clean the pan & add in the leftover oil and heat it over medium heat. Add & sauté the carrots until starting to turn soften, then add in the garlic and onion.
5. When the onions turn soft; add in the ground meat & cook until turn brown; as you cook, don't forget to break the meat into large chunks.
6. When done, season the meat with pepper, thyme & salt. Add in the peas and mushrooms. Sprinkle the mixture with flour; stir well. Add in the Worcestershire, tomato paste & the leftover wine.
7. Cook & stir the mixture for a couple of more minutes. Add in the stock & bring it to a simmer until sauce is reduced and thick.
8. Immediately remove it from the heat & stir in the zucchini. Season to taste. Pour the meat mixture into the prepared casserole. Spoon the mashed potatoes on top of the meat; spread & smooth the top.
9. Brush the potatoes with a beaten egg & then sprinkle with the Parmesan. Bake the casserole until hot & bubbling and the potatoes turn browned, for 25 to 30 minutes.

Baja Chicken Tacos

Prep Time: 15 minutes
Cooking Time: 30 minutes
Servings: 2

Ingredients

- 1 cup plain Greek yogurt
- 2 boneless, skinless chicken breasts
- 1 chipotle pepper in adobo, minced
- Corn tortillas
- 1 bag of broccoli slaw
- Chili powder, cumin, pepper & salt to taste
- 1 tablespoon honey

For Toppings:
- Avocado, Cilantro, Lime & Salsa

Directions

1. Over medium-high heat in a large skillet; heat a small amount of oil until hot.
2. Season both sides of the chicken with pepper, chili powder, cumin & salt.
3. Once the oil is hot; carefully place the seasoned chicken into the hot oil & cook for 4 to 5 minutes on both sides.
4. In the meantime; combine yogurt together with the honey, chipotle pepper & salt in a bowl; mix well. When the chicken has finished cooking, immediately remove it from the hot pan & chop into small pieces, bite-sized.
5. Place the corn tortilla over the open flame on your gas stove and let char on both sides.
6. Assemble the taco with the chicken and slaw, drizzle with the sauce& then add in your favorite toppings.
7. Serve immediately & enjoy.

Chicken Riesling

Prep Time: 20 minutes
Cooking Time: 25 minutes
Servings: 2

Ingredients

- 4 skinless boneless chicken breasts (thighs or whatever you prefer)
- 1 small onion or a large shallot, chopped finely
- 8 ounces mushrooms, sliced
- 1 cup dry Riesling
- 2 thin slices or 1 thick slice of bacon, diced
- 4 tablespoon butter
- ¼ to ⅓ cup heavy cream
- 2 tablespoon olive oil
- Pepper & salt to taste

Directions

1. Pound the chicken to make them all similar thickness, approximately ½" and then sprinkle with pepper and salt.
2. Over medium high heat in a large skillet; fry the bacon for a couple of minutes, until cooked through. Using a large slotted spoon; remove & reserve it on a large plate.
3. Add olive oil in the same skillet with the bacon dripping & fry the chicken for a couple of more minutes, until golden brown spots starts to appear; ensure that you don't burn the chicken. Remove the chicken & place it on the plate with the bacon; let rest until ready to use.
4. Add the onion or shallot and mushrooms; scraping up any brown bits from the pan. Cook for a couple of minutes, until the shallot turns translucent and golden. Add wine & bring it to a boil; continue to cook until reduces to thick syrup like consistency.
5. Add the bacon and chicken any accumulated juices to the pan again. Add in the cream & let simmer until the sauce is slightly thickened. Remove from heat; remove the chicken & add the cold butter to the hot pan, stirring the butter constantly until completely melted into the sauce. Serve the chicken with the sauce along with some buttered egg noodles.

Fish Tacos

Prep Time: 10 minutes
Cooking Time: 30 minutes
Servings: 4

Ingredients

- 1 pound halibut fillet, skin removed
- ¼ green cabbage
- 10 corn tortillas, warmed
- ¼ cup white onion, chopped
- salsa
- Juice of 1 lime, freshly squeezed
- ¼ cup English cucumber, chopped
- Guacamole
- ½ bunch of fresh cilantro, chopped
- 1 tablespoon olive oil
- Pepper & salt to taste

Directions

1. For Cabbage Slaw: In a large bowl add the chiffonade cabbage together with cucumber, onion & cilantro; squeeze the lime juice on top & toss well; sprinkle pepper & salt to taste; let sit for 30 minutes at room temperature.
2. Preheat your oven to 400 F.
3. Over medium heat in a non-stick oven proof pan; heat up the olive oil until hot and then carefully add the halibut; cook until the first side turn brown; turn over & put the pan in the preheated oven until the halibut is flakey & cooked through, for 10 to 15 minutes.
4. Flake the cooked halibut into a bowl & serve with warmed corn tortillas & the bowls of the guacamole, cabbage slaw & salsa. Enjoy.

Tuna Poke

Prep Time: 15 minutes
Cooking Time: 25 minutes
Servings: 4

Ingredients

- 1 pound ahi tuna, cut into cubes
- 3-4 tablespoon reduced-sodium soy sauce
- 1 tablespoon each of sesame seeds & sesame oil
- 2 green onion, chopped
- 1 avocado, cut into cubes

Directions

1. Combine the entire ingredients together in a large bowl; mix well & refrigerate until ready to serve.

Factory Burrito Grande

Prep Time: 10 minutes
Cooking Time: 30 minutes
Servings: 4

Ingredients

- 3 to 4 chicken breasts

Additional Ingredients:
- Black Bean Rice Mix; cooked
- 8 ounces Mexican blend cheese, shredded
- 1 large white Onion; chopped or sliced
- 8 to 10 Burrito Size tortillas
- 1 tablespoon olive oil
- Fresh cilantro, chopped

For Marinade:
- 2 tablespoon red wine vinegar
- 1 tablespoon McCormick Montreal Steak Seasoning Mix
- 2 tablespoon water
- 1 tablespoon oil

For Black Bean Salsa Topping:
- 1 medium red onion, chopped
- 2 ripe Roma Tomatoes
- ¼ cup fresh cilantro, chopped
- 1 can each of sweet corn and black beans; rinsed & drained
- ½ teaspoon salt

Suggested Extras:
- Avocados chopped
- Black bean Salsa
- Chives
- Sour Cream
- Tomatoes chopped

Directions

1. Combine the seasoning mix together with vinegar, oil & water in a large-sized shallow dish
2. Add in the chicken breasts; cover & let refrigerate for a minimum of half an hour (turning the pieces halfway through the marinating process)
3. Preheat your oven to 350 F
4. Cook or grill the chicken breasts in 1 tablespoon of olive oil for a couple of minutes, until cooked through and then chop into small, bite-sized pieces
5. Now, over medium to high heat in a large skillet; heat up the olive oil until hot. Add & sauté the onions until tender & translucent, for a minute or two.
6. Add the prepared rice mixture & chicken breasts; cook for a couple of more minutes, until heated through
7. Evenly spoon the mixture into Tortillas; rolling the tortilla and place the rolled burritos into a casserole dish, 9×13".
8. Cover burritos heavily with the shredded cheese & bake until the cheese is melted & gooey and burritos are heated through; for 20 minutes
9. In the meantime; prepare the Black Bean Salsa to serve on the top & on the side
10. Sprinkle the freshly chopped cilantro over the burritos and serve with avocados, bean salsa, any leftover rice & sour cream. Enjoy.

Chicken Madeira

Prep Time: 20 minutes
Cooking Time: 50 minutes
Servings: 4

Ingredients

- 1 pound chicken breasts (roughly 2 large pieces)
- 3 tablespoon unsalted butter, divided
- 1 ½ cup beef broth or stock; reduced-sodium
- 2 tablespoon olive oil divided
- 1 pound asparagus blanched
- 16 ounces button mushrooms; sliced thickly
- ½ medium or 1 small yellow onion; diced finely
- 2 garlic cloves, large & minced
- ½ cup regular or heavy whipping cream
- 2 tablespoon fresh parsley; chopped finely, plus more to garnish
- 1 ½ cup sweet white wine
- 1 cup shredded mozzarella cheese
- ¾ teaspoon sea salt, divided & black pepper to taste

Directions

1. To blanch the asparagus: Remove the fibrous stems from asparagus by snapping them off. Fill a medium-sized pot with approximately 6 cups of water and bring it to a boil over moderate heat and add 1 tablespoon of the salt. Add in the asparagus & let boil for a couple of minutes, until bright green & crisp tender, uncovered. Once done; remove the asparagus from hot water & set aside.
2. Now, over medium to high heat in a large, heavy (oven-safe) pan; heat 1 tablespoon of oil and 2 tablespoon of butter. Add in the sliced mushrooms & cook until soft, for 3 to 5 minutes. Stir in the diced onion & cook for 3 more minutes. Add in the minced garlic cloves then season with 2 tablespoon parsley, ¼ teaspoon black pepper & ¼ teaspoon salt. Cook for 2 more minutes and then remove the mixture to a clean, large plate; wipe out the skillet using wet paper towel.
3. Slice chicken breasts in half lengthwise & pound each cutlet between the plastic wrap until no more than ¼" thick. Season all sides of the chicken with ¼ teaspoon of black pepper and ½ teaspoon of salt. Place the same pan over medium to high heat & add 1 tablespoon of oil and 1 tablespoon of butter. When butter is done foaming; add in the chicken breasts & sauté until turn golden & cooked through, for 3 to 4 minutes per side. Remove the chicken from pan to the same plate with mushrooms.
4. Add 1 ½ cups of the Madeira in the same pan & bring it to a boil; continue to cook for 3 to 5 minutes, until decreased by half; scraping the bottom of your pan to deglaze. Add 1 ½ cups of the beef broth & boil for 8 to 10 minutes, until approximately ⅔ cup of the liquid remains. Decrease the heat to medium; add ½ cup of the cream & let simmer for 2 more minutes, until the sauce thickens. Season with pepper and salt to taste.
5. Place the chicken back to the pan; turning it several times until nicely coated in the sauce. Top with asparagus, mushrooms & sprinkle with 1 cup of mozzarella cheese. Broil until the cheese is completely melted, for 3 to 4 minutes. Remove from oven & garnish with the fresh parsley.

Chicken Bellagio

Prep Time: 15 minutes
Cooking Time: 55 minutes
Servings: 1 person

Ingredients

- 8 ounces Spaghettini pasta
- 1 teaspoon lemon juice, freshly squeezed
- ¼ teaspoon kosher salt
- 2 ea. boneless, skinless chicken breasts (3 ounces), Pounded
- ⅛ teaspoon freshly ground black pepper
- 1 ounces all-purpose flour
- ¼ ounces Romano/Parmesan cheese blend
- 2 ounces. egg wash
- ½ teaspoon fresh parsley, chopped
- 2 ounces seasoned breadcrumbs
- ¼ ounces Parmesan/Romano Cheese Blend
- 3 ounces parmesan cream sauce
- ¾ ounces prosciutto, sliced into 1/16"
- 1 ½ ounces. basil oil
- ½ ounce chicken broth
- 1 tablespoon butter
- ½ ounces baby arugula
- A pinch each of freshly ground black pepper & kosher salt
- 1 t canola oil
- ½ teaspoon olive oil

Directions

1. Fill a large pot with lightly salted water; bring it to a boil over moderate heat and drop the pasta carefully into it; cook for 6 to 8 minutes, until al dente
2. Evenly season the chicken breasts (only one side) with pepper and salt. Lightly coat both sides of the chicken with flour; shaking off any excess. Dip the chicken into the egg wash & then evenly coat both sides with the seasoned breadcrumbs; pressing the breadcrumbs gently onto the chicken to help "set" the coating.
3. Now; over moderate heat in a large sauté pan; heat up the oil until hot. Carefully place the breaded chicken breasts into the pan & cook until the chicken has turned a light, even golden brown and is crispy. Carefully flip & cook the other side until done.
4. In the meantime, heat up the parmesan cream sauce over medium heat in a small sauté pan or non-stick sauce pot set. Bring it to a boil, stirring occasionally. The moment sauce starts to boil, immediately remove it from the heat; set aside & keep it warm.
5. Ladle the basil oil & chicken broth into a large non-stick sauté pan placed over medium heat. Cook until heated through and then add in the butter; stir well to incorporate. Continue cooking until just heated through. Add the in the drained pasta & cheese; toss to incorporate.
6. Mound the pasta onto the middle of the serving platter, leaving 1" open border within the rim. Ladle 2 ounces. of the parmesan cream sauce onto the platter and around the pasta.
7. Place the chicken cutlets over the pasta at a slight angle. When platted correctly, you would be able to see a very quantity of the pasta. Drizzle the leftover parmesan cream sauce randomly on top of the chicken. Evenly sprinkle the chopped parsley on top of the pasta and chicken.
8. Set the prosciutto slices around the top of the chicken forming a fluffy "crown" with an open area left in the center.
9. Place the arugula into a clean stainless steel mixing bowl. Drizzle the oil into the bowl and over the arugula. Squeeze the lemon wedge over the arugula and season with a small amount of pepper and salt. Add the Parmesan/Romano into the bowl. Toss the ingredients gently to coat the arugula with the dressing. Mound the arugula on top of (middle) the chicken & on top of the pasta within the open area of the prosciutto crown.

Chicken & Biscuits

Prep Time: 10 minutes
Cooking Time: 30 minutes
Servings: 6 persons

Ingredients

- 1 ½ pounds boneless, skinless chicken thighs or breasts (roughly 8)
- ½ cup dry white wine
- 2 celery stalks, sliced thinly
- ½ teaspoon poultry seasoning
- 1 small onion, chopped
- ¼ cup all-purpose flour
- 6 Easy Drop Biscuits, split
- ¾ pound carrots (roughly 4 medium-sized), cut into 1" lengths
- 1 cup frozen peas
- ½ cup heavy cream
- Black pepper & kosher salt to taste
- ½ cup chicken broth, reduced-sodium

For Easy Drop Biscuits
- 1 tablespoon baking powder
- 2 cups all-purpose flour, spooned & leveled
- 1 stick (½ cup) cold unsalted butter, cut into small pieces
- 1 cup whole milk
- 1 teaspoon kosher salt

Directions

1. Toss the carrots together with celery, flour & onion in a 4 to 6 quarts slow cooker. Place the chicken on top & season with ¼ teaspoon pepper, 1 teaspoon salt and the poultry seasoning. Add the broth and wine.
2. Cover & cook on high-heat for 2 ½ to 3 hours or for 5 to 6 hours on low-heat, until the vegetables and chicken are tender.
3. Just half an hour before serving, don't forget to prepare the Easy Drop Biscuits.
4. Ten minutes before serving, add in the peas, cream & ½ teaspoon of salt to the chicken; give everything a good stir until combined well. Cover & cook for 5 to 10 more minutes, until heated through.
5. Place the bottom halves of the biscuits in shallow bowls and then top with the chicken mixture and the leftover biscuit halves.

For Easy Drop Biscuits

1. Preheat your oven to 400 F in advance. Combine flour together with baking powder, butter & salt in a food processor; pulse on high for a minute or two, until pea-size clumps form. Add in the milk & pulse again until just moistened.
2. Drop 6 large mounds of the dough (roughly ½ cup each) onto a large-sized baking sheet & bake in the preheated oven for 18 to 20 minutes, until turn golden.

Crusted Chicken Romano

Prep Time: 10 minutes
Cooking Time: 10 minutes
Servings: 2 persons

Ingredients

- 2 chicken breasts
- 1 beaten egg, large
- 2 tablespoon Romano Cheese; grated or shredded
- ½ cup flour
- 2 teaspoon water
- Pepper & salt to taste

Directions

1. Whisk the egg together with water and prepare the egg wash.
2. Pound the chicken breasts to approximately ½" thick.
3. Season the flour with pepper and salt; lightly coat the chicken breasts with the mixture.
4. Then dip into the egg wash; cover with the shredded Romano.
5. Now, over medium high heat in a large frying pan; heat up some of the oil until hot and cook the breasts until turn golden brown, for a couple of minutes.
6. Serve with pasta & a light tomato sauce. Enjoy.

Famous Factory Meatloaf

Prep Time: 10 minutes
Cooking Time: 1 hour & 25 minutes
Servings: 6 persons

Ingredients

- ⅓ cup tomato sauce
- 1 pound lean ground beef
- ½ pound each of ground veal & ground pork
- 1 cup chopped onion
- ¾ cup large-curd cottage cheese
- 2 organic eggs
- ¼ cup dry red wine
- ½ cup cheddar cheese, shredded
- 1 tablespoon Dijon mustard
- ½ cup unseasoned breadcrumbs, dry
- 1 tablespoon salt or to taste
- ½ cup green pepper, chopped
- ¼ teaspoon pepper

Directions

1. Preheat your oven to 350 F in advance.
2. Combine the entire ingredients together in a large bowl; mix well until nicely coated.
3. Transfer the prepared mixture into a 9x5" loaf pan & bake in the preheated oven for 45 to 50 minutes.

Orange Chicken

Prep Time: 10 minutes
Cooking Time: 40 minutes
Servings: 4

Ingredients

- 1 ½ teaspoon orange zest, grated
- ¾ cup chicken broth, reduced-sodium
- 8 strips of orange peel (each approximately 2" long and ½" wide)
- ¾ cup fresh squeezed orange juice
- 1 ½ pounds chicken thighs; skinless trimmed & cut in 1 ½" pieces
- 6 tablespoon distilled white vinegar
- ¼ cup soy sauce
- 8 small whole dried red chilies, optional
- ½ cup dark brown sugar, packed
- 1 tablespoon plus 2 teaspoon cornstarch
- 3 garlic cloves, pressed or minced
- 1 piece (1") ginger, grated
- 2 tablespoon cold water
- ¼ teaspoon cayenne pepper

For Coating & Frying:
- 1 cup cornstarch
- 3 large egg whites
- ¼ teaspoon cayenne pepper
- 3 cups peanut oil
- ½ teaspoon baking soda

Directions

For the Marinade & Sauce:
1. Place the chicken thighs in a one gallon zipper-lock bag; set aside.
2. Now, combine the chicken broth together with grated zest, orange juice, ginger, soy sauce, vinegar, garlic, cayenne & sugar in large-sized saucepan; whisk until the sugar is completely dissolved.
3. Measure approximately ¾ cup of the prepared mixture out & pour into the bag with chicken; press out the air as much as possible & seal the

bag; ensure that the pieces are coated well with the marinade. Refrigerate for 30 to 60 minutes.
4. Bring the leftover mixture to a boil over high heat in the saucepan.
5. Stir the cornstarch with cold water in a small bowl; whisk the cornstarch mixture into the sauce.
6. Let the sauce to simmer for a minute, until thick & translucent, stirring occasionally. Turn off the heat and then stir in the orange peel & chilies; set the sauce aside.

For the Coating:
1. Place the egg whites in a pie plate; beat using a large fork until completely frothy.
2. Whisk the cornstarch together with cayenne & baking soda in a second pie plate until combined well.
3. Drain the chicken in a large mesh strainer or colander; thoroughly pat the chicken dry using paper towels.
4. Place half of chicken pieces into the egg whites; turn to coat and then transfer the pieces to the cornstarch mixture; ensure that the pieces are thoroughly coated.
5. Place the dredged chicken pieces on a wire rack set over the baking sheet; repeat with the leftover chicken pieces.

For the Chicken:
1. Now, over high heat in straight-sided sauté pan or 11 to 12" Dutch oven; heat up the oil until hot.
2. Work in batches & carefully place half of the chicken into the oil one piece at a time; fry for a couple of minutes, until turn golden brown, turning each piece with tongs halfway during the cooking process.
3. Transfer the chicken to a paper towels lined large plate. Heat up the oil & repeat the steps with the leftover chicken.

To Serve:
1. Reheat the sauce over medium heat for approximately 2 minutes, until simmering.
2. Add in the chicken & toss gently until coated evenly & heated through. Serve immediately and enjoy.

Shrimp & Chicken Gumbo

Prep Time: 10 minutes
Cooking Time: 25 minutes
Servings: 6

Ingredients

- 1 pound chicken breast, cubed
- 2 garlic cloves, minced
- 1 cup canned tomatoes
- 3 cup shrimp stock
- 1 teaspoon dried basil leaves
- 3 bay laves
- 1 ½ cup smoked sausage, sliced
- ½ of a yellow onion, chopped
- 1 tablespoon dried parsley flakes
- ¼ cup celery, chopped
- 1 tablespoon Cajun seasoning
- 2 pound shrimp
- 1 cup heavy cream
- ¼ cup green bell peppers, chopped
- 1 teaspoon dried thyme leaves
- ½ teaspoon black pepper

Directions

1. Add the entire ingredients (excluding the rice) together in a large-sized skillet. Cook the mixture for 45 to 60 minutes over moderate heat. In the meantime; prepare the rice per the instructions mentioned on the package. Once done; place it into the large skillet, stirring every now and then to prevent burning. Serve immediately & enjoy.

Hibachi Steak

Prep Time: 10 minutes
Cooking Time: 10 minutes
Servings: 4 persons

Ingredients

- 4 Sirloin Steaks (5 ounce)
- ¼ cup soy sauce
- 3 tablespoon teriyaki sauce
- ½ teaspoon each of freshly ground black pepper & kosher salt
- 4 teaspoon olive oil

Directions

1. Over moderate heat in a large skillet; heat up the oil. Combine soy together with teriyaki sauce, ground pepper and salt in a large-sized shallow dish.
2. Coat the steaks in this prepared mixture and then carefully add to the hot skillet. Cook for 3 to 4 minutes per side. Serve hot & enjoy.

Spicy Cashew Chicken

Prep Time: 30 minutes
Cooking Time: 25 minutes
Servings: 6 persons

Ingredients

- 1 ½ pounds chicken breast cut into bite size chunks
- Seasoned rice flour
- 6 green onions cut into ¼" pieces
- Rice flour batter
- 8 ounces cashews
- Spicy soy-sherry sauce
- ⅓ cup vegetable or canola oil

For Seasoned Rice Flour:
- ⅛ teaspoon baking powder
- ¾ cup rice flour
- ⅛ teaspoon ground black pepper
- ¼ teaspoon kosher salt
- ⅛ teaspoon paprika

For Rice Flour Batter:
- ¼ cup all-purpose flour
- 1 ½ cups rice flour
- ¼ teaspoon each of ground black pepper & kosher salt
- 1 ½ cups Ice Water

For Spicy Soy-Sherry Sauce:
- 2 ounces fresh garlic, minced
- ¼ cup sherry wine
- 1 cup hoisin sauce
- ¼ cup granulated sugar
- 2 tablespoon red wine vinegar
- ¼ cup soy sauce
- 1 tablespoon Sriracha sauce
- ¼ teaspoon red chili flakes, crushed

Directions

For the Seasoned Rice Flour:
1. Combine the entire ingredients together in a large bowl; mix well.

For the Batter:
1. Mix the ingredients completely in a bowl set over ice; set aside & keep cold.

For the Sauce:
1. Mix the entire sauce ingredients together in a large bowl; combine well.

For Cooking the Dish:
1. Toss the chicken with seasoned flour in a large bowl and then add the batter.
2. Combine carefully until coated well.
3. Now, over medium-high heat in a wok or large pan; heat up the canola oil until hot.
4. Carefully add the coated chicken pieces into the hot pan & cook until crispy & turn browned, for 3 minutes per side. During the cooking process; don't forget to break any pieces apart that may stay stuck together.
5. Add in the cashews and sauce and then add the green onions.
6. Toss together until coated well.
7. Cook until the sauce thickens, for a minute.
8. Garnish with sesame seeds, crushed cashews and parsley. Serve immediately & enjoy.

Carne Asada Steak

Prep Time: 15 minutes
Cooking Time: 35 minutes
Servings: 2 persons

Ingredients

For the Marinade:
- 1 pound skirt steak
- 1 tablespoon cilantro, chopped
- Juice of 1 lime, freshly squeezed
- 1 tablespoon white vinegar
- 1 teaspoon onion powder
- 2 Serrano peppers, chopped
- 1 garlic clove, chopped
- ¼ teaspoon pepper
- 1 teaspoon Mexican oregano
- ½ teaspoon salt

For the Sauce:
- 1 can fire roasted tomatoes (14 ½ ounces)
- 1 tablespoon white vinegar
- 1 garlic clove, chopped
- 1 teaspoon sugar
- 1 jalapeno, chopped
- 1 tablespoon cilantro, chopped
- Pepper & salt to taste

For Optional Enchilada:
- 2 ounces Monterey jack cheese
- 1 corn tortilla

Directions

1. Place the entire marinade ingredients together (don't add the steak), in a food processor & buzz them up. Pour the mixture on top of the steak in a non-reactive container & let marinade for 12 to 15 minutes.
2. In the meantime; prepare the sauce by buzzing the jalapeno together with fire roasted tomatoes, vinegar, garlic, sugar, cilantro, pepper & salt in the food processor until you get your desired consistency.
3. Now, over medium heat in a pot; cook this mixture for 15 to 20 minutes, stirring constantly and ensure that you don't burn the tomatoes. Grill the steak over high heat until you get your desired doneness. Top the steak with the prepared sauce & serve.
4. Optionally roll the jack cheese inside a corn tortilla (softened in a small amount of hot oil for a few seconds) & bake until the cheese just melts. Place this enchilada over the steak before and then spoon the sauce.

Cheesecakes

Coffee & Cream Chocolate Supreme

Prep Time: 25 minutes
Cooking Time: 2 hours & 20 minutes
Servings: 12 persons

Ingredients

- 1 package of cream cheese (8 ounces), softened
- ¼ cup sugar
- 1 can sweetened condensed milk (14 ounces)
- ¼ cup melted butter
- 1 cup chocolate wafer crumbs
- ⅔ cup chocolate syrup
- 1 cup heavy whipping cream, whipped
- 2 tablespoons instant coffee granules
- 1 tablespoon hot water
- Chocolate-covered coffee beans, optional

Directions

1. Combine wafer crumbs together with butter and sugar in a small bowl; pressing onto the bottom & 1" up the sides of a 9" spring-form pan, lightly greased; set aside.
2. Beat the chocolate syrup together with cream cheese and milk in a large bowl until completely smooth. Dissolve the coffee granules into the hot water & immediately add the mixture to the cream cheese mixture. Fold in the whipped cream and then pour on top of the crust. Cover & let freeze for overnight.
3. Just 10-15 minutes before serving; remove from the freezer & carefully run a knife around the edges of the pan to loosen. Remove the sides of pan & garnish with the coffee beans, if preferred.

Original Factory Cheesecake

Prep Time: 30 minutes
Cooking Time: 1 hour & 5 minutes
Servings: 12 servings

Ingredients

For Cheesecake crust:
- ¼ cup almonds, chopped finely
- 1 cup graham cracker crumbs
- ¼ cup walnuts, chopped finely
- 1 teaspoon cinnamon
- 2 tablespoons white granulated sugar
- 1 stick butter, unsalted, melted

For Cheesecake filling:
- 16 ounces sour cream, full-fat, at room temperature
- 2 cups white granulated sugar
- 5 large eggs, at room temperature
- 2 tablespoons cornstarch
- 6 packages cream cheese, full-fat (8 ounces each) at room temperature
- 1 tablespoon vanilla extract
- ¼ cup all-purpose flour

For Topping:
- ¼ cup white granulated sugar
- 2 cups sour cream, full-fat

Directions

1. Adjust the top rack to the middle of your oven and then preheat it to 325 F.

For Cheesecake Crust:
1. Add nuts to a food processor or chop them finely.
2. Add the entire ingredients together into a large bowl; give the ingredients a good stir until combined well.

3. Press the mixture into a 10 ½" spring-form pan, lightly coated with the butter. Press the crust using a measuring cup & try to line the sides to the center of the pan edges; set aside.
4. Refrigerate for 15 to 20 minutes.

For Cheesecake Filling:
1. Beat the cream cheese in a large bowl using a hand mixer or in the bowl of a stand mixer on medium-low speed until light & fluffy.
2. Slowly add in the sugar & continue to beat until creamy and combined well.
3. Slowly add in the eggs & continue to beat after each addition until combined well.
4. Combine cornstarch with the flour & then add to the prepared batter, whisk until combined completely. Ensure that you don't over-mix the ingredients.
5. Add in the vanilla extract and then add the sour cream; beat well (scrapping the bottom and sides of your bowl, as required).
6. Pour the cheesecake batter into the prepared spring-form pan.

To Bake:
1. Place the pan into the preheated oven and bake until the center is slightly wobble & the edges are puffed & light golden brown, for 1 hour & 15 minutes. Turn off your oven & open the door of your oven; leaving the cheesecake in the oven for an hour.

To Chill:
1. Once done, remove the cheesecake from your oven & place on a cooling rack until you can easily transfer the cheesecake to a refrigerator, for 2 hours.
2. Whisk the sour cream with sugar on medium-low speed in a medium bowl until creamy & combined completely. Taste & feel free to add more of sugar, if required.
3. Spread the topping on top of the cool cheesecake using an offset spatula. Transfer to the refrigerator again & let chill for a completely day.

Cinnabon Cinnamon Swirl Cheesecake

Prep Time: 25 minutes
Cooking Time: 1 hour & 40 minutes
Servings: 8

Ingredients

- 17 rectangles graham crackers
- 1 tablespoon butter flavoring
- 3 tablespoons cornstarch
- 1 ⅓ cups raw sugar
- 5 tablespoon vegan margarine, melted
- ⅔ cup vegan sour cream
- 3 packages of vegan cream cheese, at room temperature (8 ounce)
- 1 teaspoon lemon zest
- 2 tablespoon vanilla nut & butter flavoring
- 1 tablespoon almond milk
- 3 tablespoon raw sugar
- ½ cup firm tofu
- 2 teaspoon cinnamon
- ½ cup dark brown sugar
- reserved 3/8 cup of the batter

Directions

1. Generously grease the bottom & sides of a spring form pan then line the bottom with wax paper and preheat your oven to 350 F.
2. Form the crust by melting the margarine; add in the butter flavoring, mix well & set aside.
3. Now, grind the graham crackers in a food processor and then add in the sugar; process for on high speed for a minute.
4. Combine the butter mixtures together with graham cracker in a medium bowl until incorporated well. Press the mixture to the bottom of the spring form pan; set aside.
5. Prepare the batter by blending ⅓ cup of the sugar and cornstarch with a package of the cream cheese for a couple of minutes on low. Stop; scrape down the sides of your bowl and then slowly add in the leftover cream cheese; don't forget to scrape the sides of your bowl down, as required.
6. Combine the leftover sugar with lemon zest. Increase the speed to medium & add lemon sugar into the cream cheese mixture. Add in the vanilla; scrape the sides & set aside.
7. Combine tofu with almond milk in a blender or food processor until completely smooth. Mix in tofu mixture into the batter on medium speed. Add in the sour cream; mix well & scrape the sides again.
8. Reserve approximately 3/8 cup of the batter for swirl mixture. Pour the leftover batter into the prepared pan over the crust; set aside.
9. For swirl mixture take the kept-aside batter together with cinnamon & brown sugar; combine well. Scoop a few tablespoons full of the cinnamon mixture over the cheesecake; pressing it down gently with a spoon. Swirl the cinnamon using a knife tip to.
10. Bake in the preheated oven for 60 to 75 minutes. Let cool for a few hours. Cover & let refrigerate for 4 hours more. Garnish with the brown rice syrup and chopped pecans; serve immediately & enjoy.

Reese's Peanut Butter Cheesecake

Prep Time: 8 hours & 15 minutes
Cooking Time: 2 hours & 5 minutes
Servings: 16

Ingredients

For Chocolate Cake:
- 1 ¾ cup all-purpose flour
- 1 cup buttermilk
- 2 teaspoon baking soda
- Heaping ¾ cup of cocoa
- 2 cup sugar
- 1 tablespoon vanilla extract
- 2 eggs room temp
- 1 cup black coffee hot
- ½ cup butter melted
- 1 teaspoon salt

For Cheesecake:
- 12 fun-sized Reese's Peanut Butter cups; chopped
- 1 ¼ cup sugar
- 4 packages full-fat cream cheese (8ounces each), softened
- ½ cup sour cream
- 5 large eggs, organic
- 1 can of dulce de leche (14ounces)
- 2 teaspoon vanilla extract

For Peanut Butter Butter-cream:
- 4-5 cups powdered sugar
- 1 ½ teaspoon vanilla
- ¾ cup each of butter, peanut butter & shortening

For Ganache:
- 1 cup heavy cream
- 2 cups semi-sweet chocolate chips
- 1 teaspoon vanilla

Directions

For the Chocolate Cake:
1. Line the bottoms of 2 round baking pans, 9" each with the parchment paper; coat it lightly with the cooking spray; set aside and then preheat your oven to 350 F in advance.
2. Combine the flour together with baking soda, cocoa, sugar & salt in a large bowl; mix well.
3. Slowly add in the eggs followed by the butter, buttermilk & vanilla; continue to mix after each addition until completely smooth.
4. Fold in the hot coffee and mix until a runny batter forms.
5. Pour the prepared batter into the baking pans & bake in the preheated oven for 30 to 35 minutes.
6. Remove from the oven & let cool in the pans for approximately 10 minutes then invert them onto the cooling racks.
7. Once completely cool, wrap in the saran wrap & refrigerate.

For the Cheesecake:
1. Preheat your oven to 475 F.
2. Fill large pan with approximately ½" of water & lightly coat a standard-sized spring-form pan, 9" with the non-stick cooking spray; wrap the bottom in a tinfoil.
3. Combine the cream cheese using an electric mixer in a large bowl until completely fluffy. Add in the sugar, vanilla and sour cream; continue to mix until combined well.
4. Slowly mix in the eggs (ensure that you blend well after every addition) and then fold in the chopped Reese's Peanut Butter Cups.
5. Pour into your prepared pan & place the pan in water dish.
6. Bake in the preheated oven for 10 minutes; decrease the heat settings to 350 & continue baking until the cheesecake is just set, for 50 to 60 more minutes.
7. Remove from the oven & let cool. Once done; cover & let refrigerate for overnight.
8. Once cooled; trim off approximately ½ to 1" of the top of the cheesecake to make level & then split the cake in half using a serrated knife or cake leveler. Let chill in a refrigerator until ready for use.
9. Now prepare the peanut butter-butter cream by creaming the butter together with shortening; once fluffy, immediately add in the vanilla & peanut butter.
10. Adding one cup at a time; add in the powdered sugar and continue to cream until you get your desired level of consistency; set aside.

11. Add dulce de leche to a large bowl & add some teaspoons of the milk to thin out.

To Assemble:
1. Add 1 of your layers of chocolate cake either on a cake or turntable stand & top with half of the dulce de leche.
2. Top the dulce de leche with a layer of cheesecake.
3. Spread with approximately a cup of the peanut butter-butter cream & top with a layer more of cheesecake.
4. Spread the leftover dulce de leche & top with a layer of cake as well.
5. Trip the outside of cake, if required and make it even & spread a thin layer of your peanut butter-butter cream to do a crumb coating and seal any spaces or gaps in the cake.
6. Place in the freezer until slightly harden up, for half an hour.
7. In the meantime; prepare the ganache. Add the chocolate chips to heat proof bowl & add in the heavy cream to the sauce pan; heat until it just begins to boil, over moderate heat.
8. Pour the cream on top of the chocolate chips; cover for 5 to 7 minutes.
9. Remove the cover & stir until the chocolate completely melted into the cream.
10. Let sit until slightly thickens.
11. Remove the cake from freeze & pour some of the ganache on top and spread down the sides of your cake.
12. Repeat until sides and top of cake are completely covered.
13. Place ¼ cup of the peanut butter in small bowl & heat for a couple of minutes (over medium-low heat), until liquid then drizzle on top of the cake.
14. Carefully decorate the bottom and top of your cake with the leftover butter-cream.

Lemon Meringue Cheesecake

Prep Time: 15 minutes
Cooking Time: 2 hour & 20 minutes
Servings: 8 persons

Ingredients

- 1 package (8 ounces) Cool Whip, thawed (light ok)
- 1 can sweetened condensed milk, (14 ounces)
- ⅓ cup of lemon juice, freshly squeezed
- Zest from 2 lemons, fresh or to taste
- 1 prepared graham cracker pie crust, 9"

Directions

1. Add lemon zest with lemon juice in a mixing bowl; stir well to mix.
2. Beat in the sweetened condensed milk using a whisk until the mixture is completely uniform & smooth.
3. Carefully fold in the cool whip using a rubber spatula until mixture is mixed well and uniform. Ensure that you don't deflate the Cool Whip while mixing.
4. Spoon the prepared mixture into the graham cracker pie crust & place in a refrigerator; let chill for two hours, until set.
5. Serve chilled & enjoy.

Celebration Cheesecake

Prep Time: 15 minutes
Cooking Time: 2 hours & 10 minutes
Servings: 8 persons

Ingredients

For the Cheesecake:
- 8 tablespoon unsalted butter, at room temp
- 1 teaspoon baking powder
- 16 ounces cream cheese, at room temp
- 2 large eggs
- 1 ½ ounce Cook and Serve vanilla pudding
- ½ cup sugar

For the Cake:
- ¾ cup sugar
- 8 tablespoons unsalted butter, room temp
- ¼ cup light brown sugar
- 1 large egg, organic
- ¼ cup sour cream
- 1 tablespoon vanilla
- ½ teaspoon baking powder
- ⅔ cup flour
- ¾ cup milk
- ¼ teaspoon baking soda
- ⅔ cup rainbow sprinkles
- ½ teaspoon kosher salt

For the Butter-cream Frosting:
- 6 cups confectioners' sugar
- 1 pound unsalted butter, room temp
- ½ cup heavy cream
- Food coloring

Directions

1. Lightly coat 2 standard-sized baking pans, 9" each then line them with the parchment paper and preheat your oven to 350 F in advance.

2. Beat the brown sugar together with butter and sugar in the bowl of a stand mixer until completely creamy, for a minute or two.
3. Slowly add in the egg, sour cream & milk; mix well and then add in the vanilla; mix again.
4. Add flour followed by baking soda, baking powder & salt; continue to mix until blended well.
5. Gently fold in the sprinkles and evenly divide the batter between the prepared cake pans.
6. Bake in the preheated oven until the cakes turn golden & a wooden skewer comes out clean, for 30 to 35 minutes.
7. Let the cakes to cool in the pans for several minutes and then invert them carefully into a cooling rack to completely cool.

For the Cheesecake Layer:
1. Grease a standard-sized cake pan then line with the parchment paper and decrease your oven's temperature to 325 F.
2. Lightly grease the parchment paper. Cream the sugar with butter the using the paddle attachment in the bowl of a stand mixer.
3. Slowly add in the cream cheese and continue to cream until completely smooth & incorporated. Slowly add the eggs and mix in the baking powder and pudding until blended well.
4. Pour the prepared batter into the cake pan and bake in the preheated oven until the top is just set & turn golden, for 55 to 60 more minutes.
5. Let the cheesecake cool and then cover the cake pan with a plastic wrap; foil & place in the freezer for a couple of hours, until frozen. Prepare the butter-cream when you are ready to assemble the cheesecake.
6. Beat the butter in the bowl of a stand mixer with the whisk attachment until light & fluffy. Slowly add in the confectioner' sugar until well incorporated. Add the cream & continue to beat until completely fluffy.
7. Evenly divide the prepared butter-cream into three bowls. Tint one blue, other one pink & leaving one as white. Place a cake layer on a cake plate or stand. Frost the cake layer with the blue butter-cream.
8. Remove cheesecake from freezer & remove from pan. Place the cheesecake layer over the cake layer & frost with the butter-cream.
9. Add the second cake layer over the top & frost with the white butter-cream. Top with few rainbow sprinkles and keep the cake chilled. Bring to room temperature before serving.

Salted Caramel Cheesecake

Prep Time: 15 minutes
Cooking Time: 6 hours & 15 minutes
Servings: 6 persons

Ingredients

For the Crust:
- ¼ cup light brown sugar
- 2 cups graham cracker crumbs
- ½ cup unsalted butter, melted

For the Filling:
- 2½ cup cream cheese
- 1½ cup granulated sugar
- 2 cup sour cream
- ¼ cup All-purpose flour
- 2 teaspoon Vanilla Extract
- 5 large eggs
- 2 teaspoon lemon Juice, freshly squeezed

For Caramel Sauce:
- 1¼ cup light brown sugar
- ½ cup Whipping cream
- 2 tablespoon Caramel-flavored coffee syrup
- ½ cup unsalted butter
- 1½ teaspoon flaked sea salt

Directions

1. Lightly coat a standard sized spring-form pan with the butter and then preheat your oven to 350 F.
2. For the Crust: Combine the brown sugar together with butter & graham cracker crumbs. When done; press it lightly into the prepared spring-form pan. Place in a refrigerator and let chill until completely set.
3. For the Filling: Combine the cream cheese together with flour, sugar, eggs, lemon juice & vanilla extract. Beat until completely smooth & thoroughly combined.
4. Spread the filling into the pan & bake in the preheated oven until the center is just set, for 55 to 60 minutes.
5. Let cool & then refrigerate for a minimum of 4 hours.
6. For the Caramel Sauce: Over medium heat in a saucepan; toss the brown sugar together with coffee syrup & butter. Bring the mixture to a boil and continue to heat until the sugar is completely dissolved. Add in the whipping cream & continue to heat for 10 to 12 minutes. Let cool for several minutes.
7. When you are ready to serve the cheesecake; immediately drizzle the prepared sauce & sprinkle some sea salt over the top. Enjoy.

Chocolate Hazelnut Cheesecake

Prep Time: 2 hours & 20 minutes
Cooking Time: 50 minutes
Servings: 10 persons

Ingredients

- 1 pound cream cheese, at room temperature
- 10 ounces graham crackers (approximately 2 ½ cups crumbs or 16 sheets)
- ¾ cup chopped toasted hazelnuts
- 1 jar Nutella or equal amount of chocolate hazelnut spread (13-ounce), at room temperature
- ½ cup confectioners' sugar, sifted
- 5 tablespoon soft unsalted butter

Directions

1. Break the crackers into the bowl of a food processor and then add 1 tablespoon of Nutella & the butter; blitz until the mixture begins to clump. Add in 3 tablespoon of toasted hazelnuts & continue to pulse for a minute or two more, until damp, sandy like mixture consistency is achieved.
2. Tip this into the springform pan; pressing it lightly into the base, using the back of a spoon or your hands. Place in the refrigerator; let chill and prepare the filling.
3. Beat the confectioners' sugar together with cream cheese until smooth & soft, then patiently scrape the rest of the Nutella out of its jar and into the cream cheese mixture; continue to beat until combined well.
4. Remove the pan from the refrigerator; scrape & smooth the Nutella mixture carefully over the cracker crumb base & scatter the leftover chopped hazelnuts on top; ensure that it's covered well. Place the pan into the refrigerator again for overnight.
5. For best results; serve the cheese cake directly from the refrigerator; un-springing the cake from pan, still on its base, just before you eat. To cut it, dip a sharp knife in cold water, wiping it and dipping again between each cut. And don't worry, it may look disappointingly flat when whole, but when sliced, its dark depths are revealed.

Oreo Dream Extreme Cheesecake

Prep Time: 30 minutes
Cooking Time: 4 hours & 10 minutes
Servings: 12 persons

Ingredients

For Chocolate Later Cake:
- 9 tablespoons granulated sugar
- ½ teaspoon baking powder
- 1 large egg
- ½ teaspoon vanilla
- 1 tablespoon shortening
- ¼ teaspoon baking soda
- 2 tablespoon vegetable oil
- ½ cup all-purpose flour
- 3 tablespoons Hershey's cocoa powder (not dark)
- ¼ cup water
- Chocolate icing
- ¼ teaspoon salt

For Oreo Cheesecake Layer:
- 16 ounces softened cream cheese
- 1 teaspoon vanilla extract
- ½ cup granulated sugar
- 1 ½ cups heavy cream
- Oreo cookies, original flavor (not double stuffed)

For Oreo Mousse Layer:
- ¼ ounce (0.5) package unflavored gelatin
- 10 Oreo cookies, crushed
- 1 egg yolk
- 2 ounces white baking chocolate
- 1 ½ cups heavy cream
- 1 tablespoon milk
- 1 ½ teaspoons honey or 1 ½ teaspoons corn syrup
- ½ cup hot water

For Chocolate Ganache Layer:

- ½ teaspoon vanilla extract
- 6 ounces mini chocolate chips (½ bag)
- ¾ cup heavy cream
- 1 large egg
- ¼ cup granulated sugar
- 1 ¼ cups semi-sweet chocolate chips

Directions

1. Preheat your oven to 350 F.
2. For the Chocolate Cake: Combine the egg together with vanilla & sugar in a medium-sized bowl; mix it with an electric mixer for 2 minute on high speed. Add in the shortening and oil; mix well and then add the water; continue to mix until completely smooth.
3. Combine the flour together with baking soda, baking powder, cocoa powder & salt in a separate medium-sized bowl. Pour this dry blend into the bowl with the wet ingredients; continue to mix until completely smooth. Pour into a 10" spring-form pan, greased- well & bake into the preheated oven for 20 to 25 minutes.
4. In the meantime, prepare the chocolate icing. Once the cake is cool completely, spread the icing on top of the cake; reserving some for garnish purpose the cake later on. Freeze the cake with icing for an hour.
5. Make the Oreo cheesecake layer by combining the heavy cream together with vanilla & sugar with an electric mixer in a medium-sized bowl on high for a couple of minutes, until the cream forms stiff peaks. Mix in the softened cream cheese and continue to beat until completely smooth. Spread approximately ⅓ of the mixture on top of the icing. Place the whole Oreo cookies across the entire cake in a single layer. Follow with the leftover cheesecake mixture & let chill for an hour.
6. Prepare the Oreo mousse layer by combining ½ packet of the powdered gelatin with hot water & refrigerate until just set.
7. Once done, place into the cold water to soften the gelatin enough to loosen it from the pan. Place the softened gelatin into a double boiler & melt.
8. Carefully melt the chocolate in a separate double boiler; ensure that you don't burn it. Add the melted chocolate into the gelatin & mix well.
9. Using your hands; whip the egg yolks into a small-sized bowl until soft foamy peaks. In the meantime, bring honey to a boil. Pour the hot

honey over the yolks, stirring frequently. Fold the melted chocolate into the yolk mixture and over moderate heat in a small saucepan; heat the milk. Stir the hot milk into the chocolate mixture.
10. Whip the cream until soft peaks form in a large bowl & then fold into the chocolate mixture. Add in the crushed Oreos to the mixture; mix well.
11. Pour enough mousse on top of the cheesecake layer to form a layer approximately ½" thick. Let chill for 2 hours or for overnight.
12. Prepare the chocolate ganache layer by whisking the egg together with sugar & cream in a medium-sized metal bowl. Set the bowl on top of the water that is simmering in a medium saucepan over medium/low heat & whisk until thick, for 4 to 6 minutes. Remove the bowl from heat, add in the chocolate chips & continue to mix using a spoon until completely smooth. Spread on top of the Oreo mousse layer. Let chill for an hour.
13. Load the kept-aside chocolate icing into a piping bag. Remove the cake from springform pan & pipe the icing into 12 even circles around the side of the cake. Lay ½ Oreo cookie with the cream filling removed back onto each mound of icing.
14. Press the mini chocolate chips around the sides of your cake. Firmly press so that the chips stick and let chill for an hour more, then cut the cake into 12 slices using a serrated knife.
15. Serve with a mound of whipped cream & Oreo cookie pieces to the side. Enjoy.

Toasted Marshmallows S'mores Galore

Prep Time: 15 minutes
Cooking Time: 2 hours & 20 minutes
Servings: 8

Ingredients

- 2 cups light corn syrup
- 3 egg whites
- 2 cups powdered sugar
- ½ teaspoon salt

For the Flourless Cake
- 8 tablespoon butter (1 stick)
- 4 ounces bittersweet chocolate chips
- ½ cup unsweetened cocoa powder.
- 3 eggs
- ¾ cup sugar

For the Chocolate Cheesecake Layer
- 1 pound softened cream cheese, at room temperature
- ½ cup sugar
- 3 large eggs
- ½ cup semisweet chocolate chips, melted & cooled a bit

For the Mousse Layer
- 2 cups heavy cream
- 1 ¼ cups semi-sweet chocolate chips, melted in microwave & cooled a bit

For the Glaze:
- 1 cup butter
- 12 ounces chocolate chips
- 1 tablespoon light corn syrup

Directions

1. Lightly grease a standard sized spring-form pan, 9" and then preheat your oven to 350 F.
2. In a microwave, melt 4 ounces of bittersweet chocolate chips together with the 8 tablespoons of the butter.
3. Once done, stir in 3 eggs & ¾ cup of sugar; whisk well.
4. Add ½ cup of the unsweetened cocoa powder and then pour into the prepared spring-form; set aside and prepare the cheesecake layer.

For Chocolate Cheesecake Layer
1. Beat the cream cheese for a couple of minutes, until completely lightly & fluffy. Add sugar; mix well and then slowly add in the eggs. Pour in the cooled melted chocolate & mi to blend all. Carefully spread on top of the flourless cake layer. Bake in the preheated oven for 55 to 60 minutes. Let it cool for a couple of minutes & then let chill in the fridge for a couple of hours.

For the Mousse Layer:
1. Beat the cream in the mixer until soft peaks start to appear. Add the chocolate & mix until thick and just combined. Spread on top of the chilled cheesecake & let chill while you prepare the glaze.

For the Glaze:
1. Melt the butter and chocolate in the microwave until completely melted. Stir in the corn syrup & let cool down a bit then pour on the cake. Pour on; spread & let chill. Remove the cake from the fridge a couple of minutes before serving. Cut with a hot knife & clean knife between the slices.

For Marshmallow Topping:
1. Beat the egg whites together with corn syrup & salt in a mixer. Beat until doubled, for 5 minutes, on high speed. Add the powdered sugar and continue to beat but on low speed this time. Place some in a piping bag & pour over each slice of cheesecake you are serving. Toast the marshmallow quickly using a creme brulee torch.

Godiva Chocolate Cheesecake

Prep Time: 15 minutes
Cooking Time: 15 minutes
Servings: 1 Cheesecake

Ingredients

For Chocolate Cake:
- 1 cup butter
- 4 large eggs, separated
- 1 cup sugar
- 1 teaspoon vanilla
- 1 cup Godiva melting chocolate

For Cheesecake Filling:
- 3 large eggs
- ½ cup Godiva melting chocolate
- 1 pound cream cheese, softened to room temperature
- ½ cup sugar

For Mousse:
- 2 cups cold heavy cream
- 1 ¼ cups Godiva melting chocolate

For Ganache:
- 1 cup Godiva melting chocolate
- ½ teaspoon vanilla
- 1 or 2 tablespoons sugar
- ½ cup heavy cream
- 1 tablespoon butter

For Optional Toppings:
- Whipped cream
- 1 square of Godiva chocolate for each slice

Directions

For the Cake:
1. Grease a standard-sized cake pan, 9" and then preheat your oven to 350 F. Now, For the flourless cake: in a double boiler; melt the chocolate with vanilla butter. Beat the egg yolks with ½ cup of sugar. Fold the chocolate mixture into the egg yolks.
2. Beat the egg whites until completely frothy. Slowly add in the leftover sugar; beat to a stiff peak and then fold in the egg whites.

For the Filling:
1. Begin the cheesecake filling by melting the chocolate in a double boiler. Now, in a large bowl; beat the leftover ingredients together until completely smooth. Pour the prepared cake batter into the cake pan & carefully top with the cheesecake batter. Bake in the preheated oven until firm, for 45 to 50 minutes. Let chill in a refrigerator for 4 hours.

For the Mousse:
1. Melt the chocolate in a double boiler. Once done; immediately remove from the heat and let cool. Beat the cream until thick and then beat in the melted chocolate; continue to beat until soft peaks form. Layer the mousse on top of the cheesecake & chill.

For Ganache:
1. Begin the ganache by adding the butter and chocolate to a food processor. Boil the cream with sugar and then add the mixture into the food processor. Add vanilla & process again. Refrigerate until the ganache is spreadable then, spread on top of the cake. Refrigerate until chilled. Top with the whipped cream & a chocolate square; serve immediately & enjoy.

Ultimate Red Velvet Cheesecake

Prep Time: 3 hours & 30 minutes
Cooking Time: 1 hour & 20 minutes
Servings: 16 persons

Ingredients

For the Cheesecake:
- 16 ounces cream cheese, at room temperature
- 2 large eggs
- ⅔ cup granulated white sugar
- 1 teaspoon vanilla extract
- ⅓ cup each of heavy whipping cream & sour cream
- A pinch of salt

For the Red Velvet Cake:
- 2 ½ cups all-purpose flour
- 1 ½ teaspoons baking soda
- 3 tablespoon cocoa powder, unsweetened; not Dutch process
- 1 ½ cups granulated white sugar
- 2 large eggs at room temperature
- 1 ½ cups vegetable oil
- 2 teaspoon vanilla extract
- 1 cup buttermilk
- 2 teaspoon white vinegar
- ¼ cup red food coloring (two 1 ounce bottles)
- 1 teaspoon salt

For Cream Cheese Frosting:
- 16 ounces cream cheese, at room temperature
- 2 ½ cups powdered sugar; lightly sifted to remove any lumps
- 1 tablespoon vanilla extract
- ½ cup unsalted butter, at room temperature

For Garnish:
- White chocolate

Directions

For the Cheesecake Layer:
1. Preheat your oven to 325 F in advance. Place a large-sized roasting pan on the lower third rack of your oven. Place a kettle of water on the stove to boil. Lightly coat a standard sized spring-form pan, 9" with the nonstick spray & line the bottom with a round of parchment paper. Wrap a double layer of foil around the bottom and up the sides of the pan.
2. Mix the cream cheese using an electric mixer in a large bowl; blend until completely smooth & creamy. Mix in sugar & salt; blend for 2 minutes, scraping down sides of your bowl, as required. Slowly add in the eggs; don't forget to blend after each addition then, mix in the whipping cream, sour cream & vanilla. Mix until completely smooth.
3. Pour the batter into the prepared pan; set the pan into the roasting pan into your preheated oven. Carefully pour the hot water from your kettle into the roasting pan. Pour enough water so that there is approximately an inch of water coming up the foil along the sides of the cheesecake pan.
4. Bake in the preheated oven until set but not jiggly, for 40 to 45 minutes. Remove the cheesecake from roasting pan & let cool for an hour on a wire rack. When done, place the pan into the freezer & freeze for a couple of hours, until completely freeze.

For the Red Velvet Cake Layers:
1. Grease & flour 2 round metal baking pans, 9" each and then preheat your oven to 350 F in advance.
2. Whisk the flour together with baking soda, cocoa powder, sugar & salt in a large bowl. Slowly add in the eggs followed by buttermilk, food coloring, oil, vinegar and vanilla to the flour mixture. Beat for a minute on medium-low speed using an electric mixer until blended well; scrapping the bottom and sides of your bowl with a rubber spatula, as required. Beat for 2 more minutes on high speed.
3. Evenly spread the batter into the prepared pans and divide it equally. Bake until a toothpick comes out with a few moist crumbs attached, for 30 to 35 minutes. Let cool on a wire rack in pans for 10 minutes. Run a knife around the edge of the pans and then invert the cakes onto a rack to completely cool.

For the Cream Cheese Frosting:
1 Beat the powdered sugar together with cream cheese, vanilla & butter on medium-high speed using an electric mixer in a large bowl until completely smooth & creamy.

To the Assemble Cake:
1. Place a cake layer into the middle of a platter or cake plate. Remove the cheesecake from the freezer, take off the sides of the pan & slide a knife under the parchment to remove the cheesecake from the pan. Peel off the parchment.

2. Measure your cheesecake layer against the cake layers.
3. Place the cheesecake layer on top of the first cake layer. Place the 2nd cake layer on top of the cheesecake.

For Frosting:
1. Apply a crumb coat layer to the cake- use a long, thin spatula to cover the cake completely with a thin and even layer of frosting. Be sure to wipe off your spatula each time you are about to dip it back into the bowl to get more frosting.
2. When your cake has a thin layer of frosting all over it, place it into the refrigerator for 30 minutes to "set" the frosting.
3. Once the first layer of frosting is set, apply the 2nd layer. Start by adding a large scoop of frosting onto the top of the cake. Use a long, thin spatula to spread the frosting evenly across the top and then spread it down the sides of the cake too.
4. Decorate with white chocolate shavings. Once done, keep refrigerated until ready to serve.

White Chocolate Raspberry Truffle

Prep Time: 20 minutes
Cooking Time: 1 hour & 20 minutes
Servings: 24

Ingredients

For the Crust:
- 1 ½ cup finely crushed OREO cookie crumbs 20-30 cookies, filling removed
- ⅓ cup unsalted butter melted

For Raspberry Sauce:
- 10 ounces fresh raspberries washed & rinsed
- ¼ cup granulated sugar
- 2 tablespoon lemon juice

For Cheesecake Filling:
- 4 pkgs. (8 ounces each) Philadelphia cream cheese, at room temperature
- 1 ¼ cup granulated sugar
- 5 eggs room temperature
- ½ cup sour cream room temperature
- 4 ounces white chocolate roughly chopped
- 2 teaspoon vanilla

For Garnish:
- 2 ounces white chocolate shaved
- ½ cup powdered sugar
- 1 cup heavy whipping cream

Directions

1. Prepare a standard-sized roasting pan with an oven bag to surround the spring-form pan.

For the Crust:
1. Remove the filling from the Oreo cookies and process them in a food processor for half a minute, until fine. Ensure that there are no larger pieces of the cookies.
2. Mix the Oreo cookie crumbs together with the melted butter.
3. Press the cookie mixture into a standard-sized spring form pan, 9". Press the crumb mixture flat into the bottom using the bottom of a drinking glass & partially up the sides of the spring--form pan. Transfer the crust to the freezer and prepare the filling & raspberry sauce.

For the Raspberry Sauce:
1. Add the raspberries, lemon juice and sugar in a medium-sized saucepan. Bring everything together to a boil & let simmer until the raspberries are completely dissolved, stirring frequently.
2. Remove the seeds through straining the sauce into a bowl; set aside & let cool and prepare the cheesecake filling.

For the Cheesecake Filling:
1. Combine the softened cream cheese together with the vanilla, sugar & sour cream using the paddle attachment in the bowl of a stand mixer. Mix for a couple of minutes, until completely smooth & creamy on high speed; scraping down the sides of your bowl, as required.
2. Slowly add in the eggs with the mixer still running on medium speed. Blend on high until the filling is smooth and the eggs have incorporated well.

To Assemble the Cheesecake:
1. Preheat your oven to 475 F in advance. Place an oven-safe roasting pan or large pan & the oven bag filled with approximately ½" of water into the oven.
2. Chop the 4 ounces of white chocolate into the coarse chunks. Remove the crust from freezer & sprinkle white chocolate chunks onto the bottom of the crust.
3. Pour half of the cheesecake filling over the white chocolate and smooth until even using a large rubber spatula.
4. Drizzle approximately ¼ cup of the raspberry sauce on top of the surface. Swirl the raspberry sauce into the cheesecake filling using a butter knife.
5. Pour the leftover filling into the pan.
6. Drizzle a couple tablespoons more of the raspberry sauce on top of the cheesecake & swirl. Refrigerate the remaining sauce. Carefully place the cheesecake into the water bath in the oven.
7. Bake in the preheated oven for 10 to 12 minutes, then decrease your oven's heat to 350 F & bake until the top of your cheesecake turns a light brown color, for 60 more minutes.
8. When cooled; using a plastic wrap; cover the cheesecake & place in refrigerator; let chill for overnight.

To Prepare Cheesecake for Serving
1. Shave the leftover white chocolate. Sprinkle the entire top surface of the cooled cheesecake the white chocolate shavings.
2. Make the whipped cream by whipping the powdered sugar and heavy cream until completely fluffy, for 5 to 6 minutes on high speed in a stand mixer.
3. Pipe the fresh whipped cream along the edges of the cheesecake. Garnish with the raspberries.
4. Slice; serve & enjoy.

Key Lime Cheesecake

Prep Time: 20 minutes
Cooking Time: 1 hour & 30 minutes
Servings: 10

Ingredients

- 1 cup graham cracker crumbs
- 2 ½ tablespoon unsalted butter, at room temperature
- 1 ½ cups plus 1 ½ tablespoon sugar
- 5 large eggs
- Zest from 1 lemon
- 2 ½ pounds cream cheese, softened
- ½ cup sour cream
- 3 tablespoon all-purpose flour
- Zest from 1 lime
- 2 egg yolks
- ½ teaspoon vanilla extract

For Frosting:

- 1 ½ teaspoon Key lime zest
- ½ cup butter, softened
- 1 teaspoon vanilla extract
- 16 ounces powdered sugar
- 1 to 2 tablespoon milk
- 3 tablespoon Key lime juice
- ⅛ teaspoon salt

Directions

1. Preheat your oven to 375 F in advance.
2. Lightly coat the bottom of a large sized spring-form pan with butter.
3. For the Cake Crust: Combine the cracker crumbs together with 1 ½ tablespoons of sugar and butter in a large bowl. Press the mixture onto the bottom of the pans & bake in the preheated oven until turn browned. Set the pan aside and let cool. Once done; lightly coat the sides with the butter.
4. Decrease your oven's temperature to 350 F.
5. For the Cake Filling: Combine cream cheese together with zests, 1 ½ cups of sugar & vanilla extract in a large bowl. Beat with a mixer for a minute or two, until light & creamy. Mix in the flour & then mix in the eggs and more of egg yolks. Finally, mix in the sour cream until filling smooth and then, pour the mixture over the crust.
6. Wrap the pan in foil & place in a large-sized roasting pan halfway full of hot water. Bake in the preheated oven for 1 hour & 30 minutes. Once done; remove the cake & refrigerate for overnight.
7. Just before serving: Beat the entire frosting ingredients together in a large-sized bowl using an electric mixer for a minute or two, until creamy & fluffy; then, spread on top of the cheesecake.

Chocolate Mousse Cheesecake

Prep Time: 20 minutes
Cooking Time: 1 hour & 10 minutes
Servings: 8

Ingredients

For Crust:
- 1 cup unsalted butter, at room temperature
- 4 cup chocolate cookie crumbs

For Chocolate Mousse:
- 1 teaspoon gelatin
- 1 tablespoon cold water
- ⅓ cup cocoa powder
- 1 tablespoon vanilla
- Shaved chocolate to garnish
- 1 cup whipping cream
- ½ cup sugar

For Filling:
- 4 pkg. (8 ounces each) cream cheese, softened
- 6 ounces semisweet chocolate, chopped finely
- 2 teaspoon vanilla extract
- 1 ¼ cup sugar
- 5 large eggs
- ½ cup sour cream

Directions

1. Preheat your oven to 350 F in advance. Over medium heat in a large saucepan; heat the butter until melted. Remove the melted butter from heat and then mix with the cookie crumbs in a large bowl. Press the mixture on 10" round pan & bake in the preheated oven for 8 to 10 minutes.
2. Now, over moderate heat in a small saucepan; melt the chocolate. Stir the cream cheese together with sour cream, vanilla and sugar using an electric mixer. Whisk the eggs in a large bowl & add to the mixture. Blend on high until combined well. Pour the filling on crust & bake until the top turns golden brown, for 45 to 50 minutes.
3. For the Chocolate Mousse: Combine the gelatin with 2 tablespoons of boiling water until completely dissolved. Let cool. Combine cocoa and sugar in a medium-sized bowl. Add in the vanilla and whipping cream. Using an electric mixer; blend on high until thick. Let the chocolate mousse to cool in a fridge. Once done, spread the chocolate mousse over the cheesecake use a large rubber spatula. Sprinkle the shaved chocolate on mousse & top with the whipped cream. Serve and enjoy.

Tiramisu Cheesecake

Prep Time: 1 hour
Cooking Time: 30 minutes
Servings: 10

Ingredients

For the Crust:
- ¼ cups butter, melted
- 1½ cup gingersnap cookie crumbs

For the Filling:
- 2 tablespoon unflavored gelatin
- ⅔ cup sugar
- 2 cup heavy cream, divided
- ¼ cup cocoa powder
- 4 whole large egg yolks
- ½ cup brewed espresso, cooled, divided
- 1 pound, 1-⅔ ounces, weight mascarpone cheese
- 12 pieces ladyfingers
- ½ teaspoon salt

Directions

1. Lightly coat a 9" spring-form pan with the grease. Line the side and bottom of your pan with the parchment paper; set aside and then preheat your oven to 350 F.
2. Prepare the crust by combining the entire crust ingredients together using a large fork. Press the mixture onto the bottom of your spring-form pan and bake in the preheated oven for 12 to 15 minutes; set aside until completely cool.
3. Put approximately ¼ cup of the cream in a small-sized bowl & sprinkle the gelatin on top. Let stand for 3 to 5 minutes.
4. Beat the leftover heavy cream in the bowl of a standing mixer until stiff peak forms. Keep refrigerated until ready to use.
5. Now, in a large-sized mixing bowl set over a pot of simmering water; add in the egg yolks, sugar & salt. Beat constantly using an electric hand mixer until the egg yolks turn pale yellow in color and the sugar is dissolved completely. Remove from the heat and then whisk in the gelatin mixture.
6. Beat the mascarpone on medium speed in the bowl of a standing mixer attached with a paddle attachment for 3 to 5 minutes, until light & fluffy.
7. With the mixer still running on low, slowly add in the gelatin mixture and yolk; scrapping down the bottom and sides of your bowl, as required. Mix in ¼ cup of the cooled espresso until combined well and then fold in the chilled whipped cream.
8. Pour ½ of the cheese mixture on top of the cooled crust.
9. Work in batches & soak the ladyfingers in the leftover espresso for a couple of seconds. Lay the soaked ladyfingers on top of the cheese mixture. Pour the leftover cheese mixture on top. Using an offset spatula; level the top.
10. Using a plastic wrap; cover & let refrigerate for overnight.
11. Just before serving; don't forget to top with the sifted cocoa powder.

Carrot Cake Cheesecake

Prep Time: 20 minutes
Cooking Time: 20 minutes
Servings: 6

Ingredients

For Cheesecake:
- 16 ounces cream cheese
- ¾ cup granulated sugar
- 1 tablespoon flour
- 3 large eggs
- 1 teaspoon vanilla

For Carrot Cake:
- 1 cup flour
- 2 eggs
- 1 teaspoon vanilla
- ½ cup flaked coconut
- 1 teaspoon baking soda
- A can of crushed pineapple; drained, reserve the juice (8.5 ounces)
- 1 cup grated carrots
- ¾ cup vegetable oil
- 1 teaspoon cinnamon
- ½ cup walnuts, chopped
- 1cup granulated sugar
- A pinch of salt

For Pineapple Cream Cheese Frosting:
- 1 ¾ cups powdered sugar, sifted
- 2 ounces cream cheese, softened
- 1 tablespoon reserved pineapple juice
- ½ teaspoon vanilla
- 1 tablespoon butter, softened
- A dash of salt

Directions

1. Lightly coat a 9 or 9 ½" spring-form pan with some butter; set aside until ready to use.

For Cheesecake:
1. Beat the cream cheese together with sugar in the bowl of an electric mixer until completely smooth. Beat in the flour, vanilla and eggs for a minute or two, until smooth; set aside until ready to use.

For Carrot Cake:
1. Combine the eggs together with oil, vanilla & sugar in a large bowl; thoroughly blend. Stir in the baking soda, flour, salt and cinnamon; mix well. Stir in the drained pineapple, walnuts, carrots and coconut.
2. Spread approximately 1 ½ cups of the carrot cake batter over the bottom of your greased pan. Using large spoonful's; drop the cream cheese batter on top of the prepared carrot cake batter. Top with large spoonful's of the leftover carrot cake batter. Repeat with leftover cream cheese batter, evenly spreading using a sharp, long knife.
3. Bake in the preheated oven until the cake is cooked through and set, for 60 to 65 minutes. Let cool at room temperature and then refrigerate.
4. Combine the for pineapple cream cheese frosting ingredients together in the bowl of an electric mixer. Beat until smooth & you get spreading like consistency. Frost the top of your cold cheesecake.
5. Refrigerate for a couple of hours; serve and enjoy.

Pumpkin Pecan Cheesecake

Prep Time: 20 minutes
Cooking Time: 20 minutes
Servings: 9

Ingredients

For Glazed Pecans:
- ½ teaspoon cream of tartar
- 3 cup sugar
- Perfect pecan halves
- 1 cup water

For Pecan Filling:
- 1 teaspoon vanilla
- 3 large eggs
- 1 graham cracker crust
- 3 tablespoon butter, melted
- 1 cup dark corn syrup
- ½ cup sugar

For Pumpkin Cheesecake Filling:
- 1 cup sugar
- 2 ½ pounds cream cheese
- 1 pound (1 can) mashed pumpkin
- 4 large eggs, lightly beaten
- 1 cup heavy cream
- 3 egg yolks, lightly beaten
- 1 teaspoon ground ginger
- 2 tablespoon all-purpose flour
- 1 teaspoon ground cloves
- 2 teaspoon ground cinnamon
- 1 tablespoon vanilla

Directions

For Glazed Pecans:
1. Over moderate heat in a saucepan; combine cream of tartar together with sugar & water until the sugar is completely dissolved, stirring frequently & scraping the sides to get rid of any sugar crystals. Cook until crisply when dropped from a spoon, don't stir.
2. Stick into a pecan half using a long sharp pin & then dip into the sugar. Place them on a piece of buttered wax paper and let cool until harden; set aside until ready to use.

For Pecan Filling:
1. Preheat your oven 350 F in advance.
2. Combine eggs together with sugar, melted butter, vanilla & corn syrup in a medium bowl. Pour the batter into a 10" graham cracker crust, spring form pan and then cover with the pecans. Bake in the preheated oven until the filling is somewhat firm, but not completely cook, for 20 minutes. Remove from the oven & place it on a wire rack.

For Pumpkin Cheesecake Filling:
1. Preheat your oven 425 F.
2. Beat the cream cheese together with sugar, eggs & yolks in a large bowl.
3. Add in the flour, ginger, cloves & cinnamon.
4. Beat in the vanilla and cream and then add the mashed pumpkin; continue to beat using an electric mixer at medium speed, until combined thoroughly.
5. Pour the mixture on top of the pecan layer & bake for 12 to 15 more minutes. Decrease your oven's temperature to 275 F & bake for an hour more. Turn off the heat; leaving the cake in the oven for overnight.
6. Top the cake with the glazed pecans; ensure that you make circles from the outside and then another one inside the first row, repeating to the middle of the cake. Make whipped cream rosettes around the outside of the cake. Serve and enjoy.

Specialty Desserts

Warm Apple Crisp

Prep Time: 25 minutes
Cooking Time: 50 minutes
Servings: 12

Ingredients

For Filling:
- 4 teaspoon all-purpose flour
- ⅓ cup packed light brown sugar
- 1 tablespoon fresh lemon juice
- 4 granny smith apples, large, peeled & cut into 3/8" slices
- 1 tablespoon light butter cut into pieces cold
- ½ teaspoon ground cinnamon

For Topping:
- ¼ cup flour
- 3 tablespoon light butter cold cut into pieces
- 1 cup vanilla ice cream, low-fat
- ⅓ c each coarsely chopped walnuts, old fashioned rolled oats, and packed light brown sugar
- 1 cup non-dairy whipped topping, fat-free
- ¼ teaspoon ground cinnamon
- 4 teaspoon caramel topping, fat-free

Directions

1. Lightly coat an 8" square baking pan with the cooking spray and preheat your oven 350 F in advance.
2. Combine flour together with sugar & cinnamon in a large bowl. Add in the apples & lemon juice; toss to evenly coat. Mound the filling into the prepared baking dish dot with the butter cut into bits.
3. Bake in the preheated oven for 20 to 25 minutes. Remove and let cool on wire rack. Increase your oven's temperature to 375 F.
4. Toss flour, oats, walnuts, sugar and cinnamon in a large bowl. Add butter rub in with the fingers until crumbly and evenly moistened.
5. Evenly sprinkle the topping on top of the apples; lightly pressing it down. Place the dish into the oven & bake until the filling is bubble, crisp & browned, for 20 to 25 minutes.
6. Let cool on wire rack until just warm and then serve with ¼ cup of ice cream, ¼ whipped topping & drizzle some caramel.

Lynda's Fudge Cake

Prep Time: 10 minutes
Cooking Time: 50 minutes
Servings: 8

Ingredients

For Chocolate Fudge Cake:
- 2 cups sugar
- 1 ¾ cups flour
- 2 large eggs
- 1 ½ teaspoons baking powder
- 1 cup milk
- ¾ cup unsweetened cocoa powder
- 1 ½ teaspoons baking soda
- 2 teaspoons vanilla
- 1 cup boiling water
- Chocolate Ganache
- ½ cup vegetable oil
- Chocolate sprinkles or chopped toasted pecans or almonds
- 1 teaspoon salt

For Chocolate Ganache:
- 2 (12 ounces each) packages semisweet chocolate chips (approximately 4 cups)
- 2 teaspoons vanilla
- 3 tablespoon cut up butter
- 2 cups whipping cream

Directions

1. Preheat your oven to 350 F in advance. Combine the flour together with cocoa, sugar, baking powder, baking soda & salt in a large-sized mixer bowl.
2. Beat in eggs with milk, vanilla and oil on medium speed using an electric mixer; beat for a minute or two. Decrease the speed to the lowest and then beat in the boiling water until blended well.
3. Pour the prepared batter into 2 lightly greased 9" round layer cake pans, dividing the batter evenly between the pans.
4. Bake for 30 to 35 minutes. Let cool in the pans for 15 to 20 minutes and then remove to racks to completely cool.
5. When cool, cut each layer horizontally in half with a long serrated knife. Spread a layer of Chocolate Ganache over the bottom layer & over tops of 2 more cake layers; stack them together on a large-sized serving plate. Place the leftover cake layer over the cake stack. Frost the sides and top of cake with the Chocolate Ganache. Press the nuts or chocolate sprinkles into the ganache around sides of cake, if desired. Refrigerate the cake until ready to serve.
6. Combine the chocolate chips with whipping cream in a large micro safe bowl.
7. Heat on high power in the microwave oven for a minute or two. Remove, stir the chocolate until melted & the mixture is blended well. Add vanilla and butter, continue to stir until the mixture is blended well & butter is completely melted.
8. Cool in a refrigerator until you get good spreading like consistency, stirring occasionally. Use to fill & frost the sides and top of a 4-layer 9"cake.

Blackout Cake

Prep Time: 1 hour & 35 minutes
Cooking Time: 1 hour & 15 minutes
Servings: 12

Ingredients

For Pudding:
- 1 ½ cups whole milk
- 2 tablespoons cornstarch
- ½ cup sugar
- 3 ounces semisweet chocolate, chopped
- 1 teaspoon vanilla extract
- ¼ teaspoon salt

For Cake:
- 1 ½ cup all-purpose flour
- ½ teaspoon baking soda
- 1 cup packed brown sugar
- 2 teaspoon baking powder
- 1 cup sugar
- ½ cup unsalted butter, cubed
- 1 cup strong brewed coffee
- ¾ cup Dutch-processed cocoa
- 1 cup buttermilk
- 2 large eggs
- 1 teaspoon vanilla extract
- ½ teaspoon salt

For Frosting:
- 8 ounces semisweet chocolate, chopped
- 2 teaspoon light corn syrup
- ½ cup unsalted butter, cubed
- 2 teaspoon vanilla extract
- ⅓ cup hot water

Directions

1. Combine cornstarch together with sugar & salt over moderate heat in a small, heavy saucepan. Whisk in the milk; cook until thickened & bubbly, stirring frequently. Decrease the heat to low & cook for 2 more minutes, stirring frequently. Stir in the chocolate until completely melted. Transfer to a large-sized bowl and then stir in the vanilla. Let slightly cool, stirring every now and then. Press the plastic wrap onto surface of pudding. Cover & let refrigerate until cold, for 2 hours.
2. Line the bottoms of two greased 8" round baking pans with the parchment paper; grease the paper lightly and then preheat your oven to 325 F.
3. Whisk flour together with baking soda, baking powder & salt in a small bowl. Now, heat the butter over medium heat in a large saucepan until completely melted. Add in the cocoa; cook & stir until blended well. Stir in the sugars. Immediately remove the pan from heat and then stir in the buttermilk, vanilla and coffee. Slowly whisk in the eggs until blended well. Stir in the flour mixture until just combined.
4. Transfer the prepared batter to the pans & bake until a toothpick comes out clean, for 35 to 40 minutes. Let cool in the pans for 10 minutes and then transfer to wire racks; remove the paper as well. Let completely cool.
5. For frosting: Melt the chocolate with butter in the top of a metal bowl or a double boiler over hot water; stir until completely smooth. Remove from the heat and then whisk in the hot water. Whisk in the vanilla and corn syrup. Refrigerate until just spreadable, for 25 to 30 minutes.
6. Cut each cake horizontally in half using a long serrated knife. Place a cake layer on a serving plate. Spread with half of the pudding. Repeat the layers. Top with a third layer of cake. Spread the frosting on sides & top of your cake.
7. Crumble the leftover cake layer; sprinkle on sides & top of cake, lightly pressing to adhere. Refrigerate the leftovers.

Chocolate Tower Truffle Cake

Prep Time: 10 minutes
Cooking Time: 30 minutes
Servings: 9

Ingredients

For the Truffles:
- 3 tablespoon, heavy cream
- 2 tablespoon flavoring of your choice (almond, orange or raspberry liqueur)
- 4 ounces chocolate, semisweet or bittersweet; cut into small pieces
- 1 tablespoon unsalted butter
- 8 fresh raspberries, optional

For the Chocolate Cake:
- 5 ounces bittersweet chocolate, cut into small pieces
- 3 large eggs, at room temperature
- 5 ounces unsalted butter, cut into small pieces
- 3 egg yolks, at room temperature
- 5 tablespoon plus 1 teaspoon all-purpose flour
- ½ cup sugar
- Ice Cream, optional
- Whipped Cream, optional

Directions

1. For the Truffles: In a small heatproof bowl placed over simmering water; combine chocolate together with cream and butter; continue to stir until completely melted. When almost melted, immediately remove from the heat & give the mixture a good stir until completely smooth. Stir in the flavoring & refrigerate for 25 to 30 minutes, until thick, stirring every now and then.
2. Line a large-sized baking tray with parchment or waxed paper. Scrape the chocolate mixture into a pastry bag attached with a #3 plain tip. Pipe 8 mounds (1" each) onto the prepared tray. Place a raspberry in the middle of each chocolate mound & pipe a small amount of the chocolate mixture to completely enclose. Refrigerate for 10 to 15 minutes, until completely firm.
3. For the Cake: Position the rack in the middle of your oven & preheat it to 350 F. Coat 8 oversize muffin cups (2" deep, 4" wide) or 1 ¼ cup custard cups with the vegetable spray or butter. Line the bottoms with rounds of waxed paper.
4. Melt the chocolate together with butter in the top of a double boiler or a small heatproof bowl placed over simmering water; let slightly cool.
5. In the meantime; beat the eggs together with egg yolks & sugar in the bowl of an electric mixer attached with beaters or a paddle on high speed for 3 to 5 minutes, until tripled in volume. Scrape in the chocolate mixture & beat until just combined, on low speed. Remove the bowl & fold in the flour using a rubber spatula. Spoon a small amount of the batter into each of the prepared cups & top with a truffle; cover with the leftover batter. Arrange the cups on a large-sized baking tray & bake in the preheated oven for 12 to 15 minutes, until the edges of the cakes start to pull away from the sides of the cups.
6. Let stand for 8 to 10 minutes. Invert onto individual dessert plates & remove the paper carefully. Serve warm. Spoon ice cream or softly whipped cream next to each cake and garnish with a few fresh raspberries, if desired. Serve immediately & enjoy.

Limoncello Cream Torte

Prep Time: 10 minutes
Cooking Time: 30 minutes
Servings: 8

Ingredients

For Torte:
- 1 teaspoon vanilla extract
- 2 cups granulated sugar
- 1 cup unsalted butter, softened
- 4 large eggs, room temperature
- 1 ½ cups self-rising flour
- 1 cup milk
- 1 ¼ cups all-purpose flour
- 1 teaspoon lemon extract

For Filling:
- 8 ounces mascarpone cheese
- ⅓ cup granulated sugar
- 2 tablespoons unsalted butter, softened
- 1 teaspoon lemon extract
- 4 tablespoons Limoncello liqueur
- 1 cup heavy whipping cream

For Frosting:
- 6 tablespoon lemon juice, freshly squeezed
- 1 cup unsalted butter, softened
- 3 tablespoon Limoncello
- 5 cups confectioner's sugar (approximately 1 pound)
- ¼ cup solid vegetable shortening
- 2 tablespoon lemon flavored gelatin

Directions

1. Lightly grease & flour 3 round cake pans (9" each) and then preheat your oven to 350 F.
2. Cream the butter and then add in the sugar; beat for 3 to 5 minutes, until light & fluffy. Slowly add in the eggs; don't forget to beat the ingredients well after each addition. Work in batches; add flour into four parts, alternating with the milk. Mix in the lemon extracts and vanilla.
3. Evenly divide the batter among the cake pans. Bake in the preheated oven for 25 to 30 minutes. Immediately remove from the pans & let completely cool.
4. Once done, pour a mixture of ¼ cup of lemon juice & 4 tablespoons Limoncello over each layer.
5. Beat the entire ingredients together for a couple of minutes, until soft peaks are formed. Evenly spread between the cooled cake layers.
6. Dissolve the gelatin in Limoncello and lemon juice. Combine the entire ingredients together at medium speed using electric mixer until desired consistency is reached. For a yellow color; don't forget to add a few drops of the yellow food coloring.
7. Keep chilled. When ready to serve; just warm for a couple of minutes. Enjoy.

Get Free Recipe eBooks!
Cookbook Club

Fabulous Free eBook Cookbooks Every Week!

Our eBooks are FREE For the first few days publication. Be the first to know when new books are published. Our collection includes hundreds of books on topics including healthy foods, diets, food allergy alternatives, gourmet meals, desserts, and easy and inexpensive meals.

Join the mailing list at:
EncoreBookClub.com

Related Copycat Books
Copycat Applebee's Recipes
http://url80.com/copycatapplebee
Copycat Candy Recipes
http://url80.com/copycatcandy
Copycat Appetizers, Vol. 1
http://url80.com/copycatapp1
Copycat Appetizers, Vol. 2
http://url80.com/copycatapp2
Copycat Buca di Deppo Recipes
http://url80.com/copycatbuca
Copycat Dessert Recipes
http://url80.com/copycatdessert
Homemade Copycat Liqueurs
http://url80.com/copycatliqueur
Copycat Olive Garden Recipes
http://url80.com/copycatolive
Copycat Panera Bread Recipes
http://url80.com/copycatpanera
Copycat PF Chang's Recipes
http://url80.com/copycatpfchang
Copycat Smoothies
http://url80.com/csmoothie
Copycat TGI Friday's Recipes
http://url80.com/fridays

Thank You for Your Purchase!

We know you have many choices when it comes to ready and recipe books. Your patronage is sincerely appreciated. If you would like to provide us feedback, go to http://url80.com/feedback.

Please Consider Writing an Amazon Review!

Happy with this book? If so, please consider writing a positive review. It helps others know it's a quality book and allows us to continue to promote our positive message. To write reviews, go to http://url80.com/reviews.

Thank You!

Made in the USA
Middletown, DE
26 August 2019